Adam Warren

David Brunner

Pat Maier

Liz Barnett

Technology in Teaching & Learning:

An Introductory Guide

KOGAN
PAGE

 Interactive Learning Centre

London ● Stirling (USA)

First published in 1996 by the Interactive Learning Centre, University of
Southampton
This edition published in 1998

Kogan Page Limited
120 Pentonville Road
London N1 9JN
and
22883 Quicksilver Drive
Stirling, VA 20166, USA

© Adam Warren, David Brunner, Pat Maier and Liz Barnett, 1998

British Library Cataloguing in Publication Data
A CIP record for this book is available from the British Library.
ISBN 0 7494 2515 6

Typeset by Kogan Page
Printed and bound in Great Britain by Biddles Ltd, Guilford and King's Lynn

Contents

Foreword

The inclusion of learning technologies within education at all levels is becoming a reality; it is something institutions, departments and individual members of staff cannot ignore. Learning technologies have opened up a world of multimedia resources that can be quickly searched and flexibly accessed across computer networks, not only locally but also worldwide. In addition, they can be combined within the rapidly growing world of communications via email, conferencing systems and the World Wide Web.

The infrastructure for these 'new' worlds is already being established in many areas of society, and we shall see an explosion of their use within the next five years. As providers and users of these technologies, educators and students need an understanding of how they contribute to the university programme. This will inevitably lead to new methods of teaching and learning, and to an exciting debate on the educational implications of technology.

This book is a technology reference book that introduces and explains a wide range of learning technologies from multimedia PCs to the Internet and the World Wide Web. Cross references are made within this book to a further book, *Using Technology in Teaching and Learning*, which discusses how this technology can be applied in an educational setting.

Wendy Hall
Professor of Electronics and Computer Science
University of Southampton

Dr Haydn Mathias
Director
Teaching Support and Media Services
University of Southampton

Preface

The book was originally funded by HEFCE, SHEFCE, HEFCW and DENI under the Teaching and Learning Technology Programme (TLTP) and published within the TLTP programme as *Technology in Teaching and Learning: a guide for academics*.

The Teaching and Learning Technology programme (Phase1 and 2) was a large national programme from 1992–1996, with an estimated outlay of £44 million. This period focused on teaching innovation using current learning technologies, with project consortia from UK universities producing computer-aided learning packages. A promotional CD-ROM of some of the packages produced can be obtained from: TLTP, Northavon House, Coldharbour Lane, Bristol, BS16 1QD, England.

In addition to the production of material, a group of eight universities were institutionally funded to work at an infrastructural level to move the culture of their university towards an increased use of learning technologies. The Interactive Learning Centre at the University of Southampton was set up under this institutional phase of the programme.

The guide was originally conceived and designed by Dr Haydn Mathias and myself as a reflection of the learning technology staff workshops held at the Interactive Learning Centre (ILC) of the University of Southampton. The guide comprised two books: one on the application of technology to teaching and learning and the other as a technical resource on understanding the technology. The books were accompanied by a video giving an overview of the technologies and their use.

I would like to thank Leslie Mapp from the Open Learning Foundation for his constructive advice during the early stages of the design. I would also like to thank our reviewers, Dr David McConnell from the University of Sheffield and Dr Chris Colbourn from the University of Southampton, who dissected the draft and gave us good advice leading to the final product.

The video of case studies was produced by Peter Phillips from the University of Southampton. We are also very grateful to those who gave us their time and agreed to appear in the video: Dr Chris Colbourn (University of Southampton), Dr Christine Steeples (University of Lancaster), Malcolm Ryan (University of Greenwich), Dr David Fincham (University of Keele) and Dr Philippa Reed (University of Southampton).

Thanks also go out to our technical team on the original guide: for graphic design and page layout, Neil Dawes, Catherine Poupart and Claire Ausden from Teaching Support and Media Services at the University of Southampton.

We also extend our thanks to our editor, Margaret Shaw, who painstakingly went through our manuscript with a fine-tooth comb, weeding out inconsistencies and clumsy expressions.

This commercial publication of the guide is sold as two separate books: *Using Technology in Teaching and Learning* and *Technology in Teaching and Learning: An Introductory Guide*. We have had very positive feedback from users of the guide. The 'Using' book looks at the application of learning and technology while the 'Introductory' book is a reference to understanding the technology. The 15 minute video (available from Southampton University) is ideal as a training tool as it gives a quick overview of learning technologies. Feedback from those using the guide to date have said they use the 'Using' book and video as part of training material for staff, while the 'Introductory' book has been used as a back-up resource for trainers and by other staff on student teaching programmes.

Pat Maier
Educational Developer
Interactive Learning Centre
University of Southampton

Permissions

I would like to gratefully acknowledge the permissions given to use the following illustrations.

Section 4.4 Web screen Mailbase uses hypermail
Kind permission for reproduction from Mailbase.

Section 5.1 Web screen Henry Purcell
Kind permission for reproduction from the British Library.

Section 4.1 web screen Telnet page, Section 4.4.1 web screen Telnet page, Section 5.3.1, web screen Telnet page, Section 5.5.4 web screen Internet Assistant for Word
Screen shots reprinted with kind permission of Microsoft Corporation.

Section 4.3.2 Web screen Newsgroup articles, follow-ups and threads
Free Agent and Agent are trademarks of Forte Advanced Management Software, Inc.
Screen shots of Free Agent and Agent reprinted with permission from Forte Advanced Management Software, Inc.

Section 5.1 Web screen Lycos
Kind permission for reproduction from Lycos.
The Lycos 'Catalog of the Internet' Copyright=A9 1994-1997 Carnegie Mellon University.

Section 5.4.2 Web screen Internet Directories
Text and artwork copyright (c) 1996 by YAHOO!, INC. All rights reserved.
YAHOO! and the YAHOO! logo are trademarks of YAHOO!, INC.

ICONS

pencil: activity section

open book: references to other material

cross: cross references to material further in the book or its partner book

exclamation mark: please note

1 Getting material into and out of your computer

1.1 *Assessing your level of technological capability*

To assess accurately the potential value of any technological development you must first:

▲ be aware that it exists

▲ have some idea how it may be used in your own circumstances

▲ develop the skills to use it effectively (or employ someone who can!)

▲ be able to assess its effectiveness as a tool.

Activity 1A   Where do you stand now?

	No idea					No problem

1 How would you rate your ability in the following:

	No idea					No problem
▲ Set up and use a video player?	0	1	2	3	4	5
▲ Set up and use an OHP?	0	1	2	3	4	5
▲ Set up and use a computer system?	0	1	2	3	4	5

2 How would you rate your understanding of the following:

▲ IT in general?	0	1	2	3	4	5
▲ Computer software?	0	1	2	3	4	5
▲ Computer hardware?	0	1	2	3	4	5
▲ Applications of IT in education?	0	1	2	3	4	5

3 Does the idea of using IT for teaching: **Worry you? Excite you?**

	0	1	2	3	4	5

How well did you do?

Score from question 1

Less than 10	You need some basic audio-visual training.

Score from question 2

Less than 5	It may be time to get some IT skills training.
6 – 12	You have a reasonable grasp of IT.
More than 12	You're doing fine.

Score from question 3

This gives an indication of your attitude to acquiring new skills.

▲ ▲

1.1.1 Assessing your basic skills

This section is not intended as a distance learning course on educational technology: its aim is rather to illustrate ways in which you may use technology as a tool to aid teaching, so we assume that you have basic IT capability.

Activity 1B   Basic IT capability

Tick what you can do
- ▲ Use a mouse ☐
- ▲ Work in a Windows or Mac environment ☐
- ▲ Manage files on both hard and floppy disk ☐
- ▲ Format floppy disks ☐
- ▲ Load and retrieve files ☐
- ▲ Print files ☐
- ▲ Use a word processor ☐
- ▲ Use a spreadsheet/database program ☐

We are assuming that you can switch the computer on and off correctly, and load the printer with paper if necessary.

These are the minimum skills you will need to perform basic operations on a computer, and no great depth of understanding of the technology is required. Once you can tick all the items on this list, you should be able to store, edit and print notes, and maintain, sort and print class files in different ways.

1.1.2 Intermediate and higher skills

Activity 1C   Intermediate IT capability

Tick what you can do
- ▲ Everything on the basic skills list ☐
- ▲ Use a desktop publishing or graphics program ☐
- ▲ Use clip art where appropriate ☐
- ▲ Use email to communicate with others ☐
- ▲ Produce OHP materials on computer ☐
- ▲ Recognize, search for, and remove a possible virus infection ☐

Activity 1D High-level IT capability

Tick what you can do
- ▲ Everything on the intermediate skills list ☐
- ▲ Use multimedia applications where appropriate ☐
- ▲ Use CD-ROM ☐
- ▲ Access the Internet via a network or modem ☐
- ▲ Produce text, graphics, photographic and ☐
  moving images in a computer-useable format
- ▲ Computer/video conferencing ☐
- ▲ Recognize the resource implications of computer conferencing ☐
- ▲ Optimize the configuration of a computer and operating system ☐

This part of the pack aims to help you to develop your skills from the basic level by introducing and explaining the more advanced topics. You will, of course, still need plenty of practical experience in order to acquire these intermediate and higher-level skills.

1.2   Choosing a computer

There is a great deal of hype about computer and related products – Windows 95, for example – and arguments between experts about the virtues of 'their' computer system. It can therefore be difficult to know where to begin when trying to make an informed judgement about an existing or planned computer system.

Before attempting to decide which is the best computer for you, it may help to familiarize yourself with some of the jargon you are likely to meet.

1.2.1 What is a platform?

In this context, platforms are simply different computer systems: for instance, IBM-compatible computers (with an 80386, 80486 or Pentium processor) are regarded as one platform, Apple Macintosh is another, and Acorn Archimedes a third.

High-end 'workstation' computers (such as those made by Sun) are not dealt with here.

1.2.2 *What is an IBM-compatible or clone?*

This category includes any computer which is capable of running DOS (Disk Operating System) and Windows. Within this broad category, however, computers can have widely differing specifications. For example:

▲ Processors and 'clock speed', which ranges from 8MHz to 266MHz; these have a direct bearing on computer performance

▲ System memory (RAM): this can be anything from 640K (kilobytes) to 256Mb (megabytes)

▲ The video display standard (the number of colours and points on the screen), the amount and type of video memory (ranging from 1Mb to 4Mb), and whether the computer has a video processor

▲ The size of the hard disk (20Mb to 5000Mb)

▲ The size and capacity of the floppy disk drive (most now have a 3.5" high-density 1.44Mb drive)

▲ 'Add-ons' such as sound cards, CD-ROM drives and tape drives

▲ The type of operating system used – for example, DOS, Windows, OS/2, Windows 95 or UNIX.

1.2.3 *IBM-PC emulation*

Some computer systems which are not regarded as true IBM-compatibles can be adapted to run PC software (DOS or Windows). This can be done in one of two ways:

▲ *By running additional software that understands DOS or Windows and thus enables the computer to behave like a PC*
The major drawback with this method is that it makes the computer very slow (running at about 50% of the speed of a PC). However, it is a relatively cheap option since software is generally less expensive than hardware. Both Acorn Archimedes and Apple Macintosh computers will run this type of software.

▲ *By adding a PC processor*
This gives all the functionality of the PC: one processor performs the operations related to the hardware itself, while a second acts on the PC instructions. Both Acorn and Apple systems provide this facility by means of 'add in' cards that plug into the computer.

The latter option provides a more viable PC emulation, but it can cost almost as much as a new PC, and you may later need to add extra hardware.

1.2.4 Which computer should you get?

The answer to the this question will depend on a number of factors:

▲ Primarily, the software you need to run – if it will only work on only one system then that must be your choice.

▲ Departmental policy – again, your choice of computer may be made for you.

▲ Whether the computer will need to be connected to a network – not all machines can be added to a local area network (LAN), and even if you will not be on a network now, you may need to bear this in mind for the future.

▲ Price – decide what add-ons (such as a large monitor or CD-ROM drive) you need, as these all involve additional cost.

If your choice of computer is not limited by the above constraints, you may well feel bewildered by the range of computer systems available. Bear in mind also that the computer market is fast-moving and a list of specifications drawn up now is likely to be out of date within six months.

When considering buying a computer system, you should ask the following questions:

▲ Does it have the latest generation processor? (For instance, in 1996 the Pentium chip was the latest processor for a PC, and a Power PC for an Apple Macintosh)

▲ Does it have enough memory? (See 1.2.5 below)

▲ What size hard disk does it have? (1000Mb is becoming standard)

▲ Is the monitor large enough to display the screen at the resolution you require while still being readable? Does it have a graphics accelerator?

▲ Does it have the capacity to add peripherals such as a CD-ROM drive, sound card, scanner, network card, modem (or fax), tape streamer?

▲ Could it be upgraded? (Changing to a faster processor or adding a better video card may significantly improve the performance of a computer at relatively small cost.)

1.2.5 RAM, storage capacity and processor speed explained

These terms often cause confusion: RAM stands for 'random access memory', storage capacity is the size of the hard disk, and processor speed is the number of 'clock ticks' per second.

▲ RAM (typically 8Mb or 16Mb) refers to the number of memory locations, contained within chips connected to the processor, which can be accessed directly. RAM is used to hold both programs and data during a session: the contents are lost once the machine is switched off or reset.

▲ Hard disk size (for example, 250Mb or 1000Mb) describes the amount of permanent storage space which the computer has. Programs and data are stored as files on a rapidly rotating disk within the computer but, unlike data in RAM, the information is retained even when the computer is switched off.

▲ Processor speed (for instance, 33MHz) is number of 'ticks per second' of the computer's internal clock – generally, the faster, the better.

You may find it helpful to think of RAM as a computer's short-term memory, storage capacity as the size of its 'filing cabinet', and processor speed as its capability to perform tasks.

1.2.6   *How much RAM do you need?*

The amount of RAM you will need depends on what you are going to use your computer for. The following table gives an idea how much RAM is needed for different applications.

1Mb	DOS programs will run
2Mb	DOS programs will run well
4Mb	Minimum requirement for Windows 3.1
8Mb	Minimum requirement for Windows 95
12Mb	Windows 95 will run comfortably
16Mb	Minimum requirement for Windows NT file server

DOS

▲ DOS applications (such as WordPerfect 5.1 and Lotus 1-2-3) rarely need more than 1Mb RAM to run satisfactorily.

Windows/Windows 95

▲ Windows (but not Windows 95) will run with 2Mb RAM, though this leaves very little space for applications.

▲ Single applications will run with 4Mb RAM and Windows, but you could have problems if you attempt to run word-processing, spreadsheet and graphics packages all at the same time.

▲ With 8Mb RAM you can run Windows 95 with multiple applications, and cut and paste data between them.

▲ Windows 95 will run much better with 12Mb RAM.

▲ To run a computer as a Windows NT file server, you will need at least 16Mb RAM.

Apple Macintosh/Power PC

▲ The early Apple Macintosh computers (Mac Classic) would run their own software with as little as 1Mb of RAM, but System 7 requires at least 4Mb.

▲ Apple Macintosh machines which will need to run multiple applications or provide a Windows environment really need at least 8Mb RAM.

Acorn Archimedes/RISC PC

▲ For most purposes, 4Mb RAM is adequate for the Acorn Archimedes series of computers, and will provide for a basic DOS emulation.

▲ For the RISC PC, 4Mb is acceptable for native applications and Windows when a second processor is installed with its own 4Mb of RAM. If the second processor has no additional memory, then 8Mb RAM is required to run Windows applications.

1.2.7 What to avoid

▲ Systems whose major functions are all built onto one main processor board – if something goes wrong you will need replace the whole thing rather than just an interface card. Having one board also makes it more difficult to upgrade your computer, for example by adding a faster video card. Ask potential suppliers about their systems.

▲ Bundled software – more often than not, what seems like a bargain is little more than a ploy to move old or obsolete stock.

▲ Suppliers you have never heard of: your institution may have a list of approved suppliers, and you should consider these first. (However, these days there is no guarantee that even a sizeable company will be around in six months' time!)

As with making any other major purchase, ensuring that your computer is 'future proof' is extremely difficult, the hardest part being to predict what your needs will be in six months', a year or three years' time. The world of computers is ever-changing: processor power seems to double every 18 months and prices tumble all the time, so you should not be surprised to find that, in a year's time, the computer you buy today will be available at half the price.

1.3   Upgrading your computer

Not all systems can be upgraded, so you will first need to find out whether upgrading your computer is possible. The next consideration will be whether any upgrade is cost effective.

1.3.1 What does upgrading involve?

To upgrade a computer you could add any or all of the following:
- more memory (RAM)
- more storage space (a higher-capacity hard disk)
- a faster processor
- multimedia facilities (sound and CD-ROM)
- a colour monitor.

Memory

There should be no problem increasing a computer's RAM, but ensure that existing memory modules do not have to be discarded before adding more. Users of DOS-based software will gain little from adding more memory, since only a small amount of RAM is needed to run DOS programs. Windows and Apple Macintosh software will run better with greater memory capacity.

Storage

Increasing the storage capacity of a system entails either replacing the existing hard drive or adding another. If the interface (the physical connection) to the system board is out of date, you may be able to add an up-to-date interface which will allow the new drive to connect to the system, but this will involve additional cost.

Processor

Increasing processor speed usually entails removing the system board and replacing it with one that supports the faster processor. It is then a matter of hoping that everything else on the system (memory, video card, hard disk, keyboard) will work with it!
If you have a PC with, for example, a 486DX33 processor, it may be possible to replace that chip alone with a faster one, to produce an appreciable improvement in performance relatively inexpensively.

It may not be worth upgrading a computer which is more than four years old. Similarly, think carefully before trying to upgrade a computer manufactured by a company which designs and produces its own components (such as Compaq, Dell, Elonex, IBM, Viglen), as you may have difficulty finding a compatible off-the-shelf processor board with which to replace your existing one.

Multimedia (PCs)

To add a CD-ROM drive, sound card and speakers your computer will need a 'free slot' into which the card may be plugged and a 'bay' where the CD-ROM can be located. If the case will not accommodate an internal drive, it could be housed externally. Make sure that your computer is capable of handling multimedia – adding a sound card and CD-ROM drive to an aged PC may give little real benefit.

But how can you improve the sound and graphics?

▲ Good audio capability needs more than the tiny built-in speaker on the front of most systems, so you will need a pair of reasonable quality stereo speakers and, most importantly, a sound card to drive them.

▲ High quality graphics require both high resolution (small dots on the screen) and lots of colours to give realism to still images. Most modern computers have such video cards installed already.

▲ Many will have graphics accelerators (video card with a built-in processor to speed up the process of getting video on the screen) already installed. This is important if you wish to show moving images – especially if you want them to fill the whole screen.

▲ Files that contain sound and graphics require plenty of storage space so you need a cheap, reliable method of distributing such data – this is where CD-ROMs come into their own. A typical CD-ROM can store more than 650 million bytes of data (1 byte will hold 1 character), whereas a typical floppy disk will hold 1.5 million bytes. By adding a CD-ROM drive to a computer, you will have access to vast amounts of storage capability and, provided there is a sound card, you can play audio CDs too.

▲ A fast processor (the chip that does the thinking) is important. With all the data to move around the computer, you cannot expect a ten-year-old PC to perform well even if you add the latest bells and whistles – a typical processor for multimedia work nowadays would be a Pentium with a clock speed of 100MHz or better. This is perhaps the most difficult bit of a computer system to upgrade.

What can you do with…?

Item	Capability	Upgrade?
Internal speaker	On a PC you can produce a limited range of 'beeps'; a Mac will reproduce digital sounds.	Add a 'sound card' and good speakers: this will allow music and digitized sounds to be reproduced
'Standard' video card	If it will display Windows software then it has some graphics capability – the precise level depending on the actual card and monitor combination	Add a better video card: one that will allow 1024 x 768 resolution (points on the screen across and down) at 256 colours
Graphics accelerator	Needed if you want to display moving images on the screen	Add a video card with 'MPEG' (moving picture) capability
Old 8086, 80286-based machine	Unlikely that Windows will work at all	Think about replacing the whole system
CD-ROM drive	Access data on CD-ROM	If you have the space in the computer, add an internal drive; if not, then add an external CD-ROM drive

Is it worth upgrading your system or do you need to start again?
The answer to this is that it depends… Some elements of a computer system, as a rule, do not need to be changed – for example mouse, keyboard, floppy disk drive, monitor and case. The elements that you may need to change or add are the 'latest' processor, video card, audio card, CD-ROM drive, hard disk drive and memory. What you have to consider is the cost of adding those items in the second group to an existing system as opposed to selling the lot and starting again.

How do you decide?
Contact a local dealer and find out how much the upgrade would cost compared to the cost of a new system less the re-sale value of the existing system. Don't forget the cost of fitting.

1.3.2 *Is upgrading cost effective?*

To a large extent, this depends how old the computer is and how much of the original system you will retain. Often, once labour charges are included, the cost of wholesale upgrading can be almost as much as a new system. Even then, owing to some unforeseen factor in the original system, the final system may not be entirely satisfactory. If the upgrade is additional memory, a larger hard disk, a sound card or CD-ROM drive to a computer that performs acceptably well, then the upgrade is usually cost effective.

There is another consideration in terms of support and warranty – especially if there is a maintenance agreement on the system – and any relevant terms and conditions.

1.3.3 *Where can you get good advice?*

However many opinions you seek, you will find that each person you ask has their own preference and can extol the virtues of machine brand 'X' over machine brand 'Y'. Try to find a colleague who has what you may regard as a suitable machine and talk to him or her about it before you brave the sales department of your local computer dealer.

1.4   *What kinds of material can you put on the computer?*

If material can appear on a printed page or as an audio-visual source then it can be stored and reproduced in a computer system. More specifically:

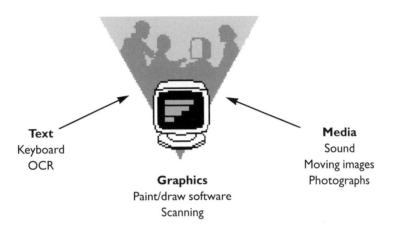

Text
Keyboard
OCR

Graphics
Paint/draw software
Scanning

Media
Sound
Moving images
Photographs

1.4.1   *Text*

The most common way of entering text into a computer is by typing it directly at the keyboard into a word processor or desktop publishing program, but this can be a considerable task if you have many years of accumulated notes to enter. You do not need to retype text which has already been typed or printed, provided the print quality is good and optical character recognition (OCR) facilities are available to scan and convert the text into a file you can then use with a word processor.

The only way in which you can really get hand-written text into a computer, at present, is as a facsimile of the written page by 'scanning' the image and storing the resulting picture of the words. Reliable OCR on hand-written text is still some way off. Work is currently under way on voice recognition for text entry: this will mean dictating text which the computer will convert into a text file for subsequent editing. The method has yet to provide a reliable, consistent way of entering text.

Technology in Teaching	1.5.1	Manual text input
Technology in Teaching	1.5.2	Scanning text
Technology in Teaching	1.5.3	Optical character recognition (OCR)

1.4.2 *Still graphics*

Assuming that the image does not exist in an electronic form already and that it is A4 or smaller in size, your starting point for transferring graphics to a computer will be one of the following:

Graphical images

▲ black and white or colour line drawings (this may include original documents)

▲ multicolour 'paint' images (16 to 256 colours or shades)

▲ photo realistic images (64,000 to 16 million colours)

For these the image source may be:
- paper (including photographs/books,
- OHP transparency
- 35mm slide
- black and white or colour negative.

For most of these a scanner will provide an effective way of transferring the data into an electronic format, provided you appreciate the limitations of such a transfer:

▲ The number of colours or shades of grey that can be reproduced depends both on the scanner and on the computer system used to display the result. This may range from 16 to 256 shades of grey or 16 to 16 million colours – depending on the type of scanner you use.

▲ The 'fineness' of the resulting image will depend on the resolution of the scanner. This may range from 300 dpi (dots per inch) to 2400 dpi – this is the number of points sampled for each inch of the picture.

▲ The size of the final file will depend on both of the above and it is important to select the optimum scanning parameters for any given image. Bear in mind that a 6" x 8" photograph scanned at 300 dpi and 16 million colours may require 4Mb of storage. A line drawing on an A4 page scanned at 600 dpi in black and white would also require about 4Mb of storage.

For 35mm negatives and slides there are low-cost scanners that will scan the media directly without having to print it first. However, the resolution is relatively low: the equivalent of 300 dpi on a 35mm slide. To provide this facility, some scanners also provide for optional film readers to be added.

Using Technology	2.3.1	Using technology to make lecture material a flexible resource
Technology in Teaching	1.5.4	Scanning graphical images
Technology in Teaching	1.5.5	Photo-CD
Technology in Teaching	1.5.6	Electronic image capture

1.4.3 Animations and video

Animations

As a rule, animations are created on the computer using software such as Autodesk Animator that will take a series of drawings and display each in turn to give the effect of a moving animation. Some of the more sophisticated packages will create 'in-between' frames automatically.

▲ The main advantage of animation sequences is their compactness when compared to video images.

▲ The main disadvantage is the expertise needed to create the original graphics to be animated.

Video

Any video source (such as a video player or camcorder) will provide a signal that can be fed into a computer through a special video capture card. This is not the same as the video display card inside the computer, but often the two are connected by a linking cable.

The purpose of the video capture card is to accept the signal from the video source, convert it into a digital form and provide a means of storing it – usually on the hard disk. Once the initial image has been captured, it may be processed further to compress the file size in order to save space. Processing can take an extremely long time, and at present there are few capture cards capable of compressing the video at the same time as capturing it.

The end result varies according to the quality of the initial signal and the capabilities of the card performing the video capture. The end result may be a Windows AVI (or Mac QuickTime) file that will display on most Windows (or Macintosh) systems without additional hardware. The clip will often be seen as a quarter-screen image unless your system has additional video playback hardware.

At present, a general guide is that one minute of video will take 10Mb of space on a disk (so a CD will hold about an hour of compressed video).

| Using Technology | 2.3.1 | Using technology to make lecture material a flexible resource |
| Technology in Teaching | 1.5.7 | Video capture and playback |

1.4.4 Audio

Playback

With the increasing popularity of multimedia applications, many systems are now supplied with sound cards which allow reproduction of MIDI files and digitized sound through a pair of external speakers (Apple Macintosh computers have long had this capability built in). Typical sound cards include the Soundblaster range and those made by Gravis, Roland and a host of other manufacturers.

Audio capture

What many users are unaware of is that these sound cards often provide audio capture facilities: with the correct software you can simply plug in a suitable microphone and digitize your own voice or tell your computer what to do! These audio snippets can be included in word-processed documents to provide audio comments in the text.

CD audio

If the computer is fitted with a CD player, you can capture audio directly from the CD – but remember that copyright still applies and that you may need permission to use the clip in a application. It is possible to obtain CDs of copyright-free music, but it is unlikely that this will offer exactly the piece you require. We discuss the actual process more fully later in this chapter.

1.5 How do you get material into the computer?

In the previous sections we considered the various forms of material we can store. In this section we consider more closely the methods available for doing so.

1.5.1 Manual text input

In considering putting text-based teaching and learning materials on computer, begin by asking yourself why you plan to type up your notes.

▲ To make them look more professional (or even legible)?

▲ In order to be able to edit, revise and update them?

▲ To prepare them for some form of computer-based presentation?

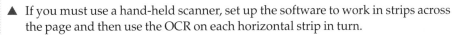

If your answers to these questions are negative, then is there any real need to type them up at all? Why not just photocopy them (again) and use more productively the time you would have spent at the keyboard?

If you do really need to transfer existing typed text into electronic format, the most cost-effective way is by OCR (optical character recognition). Scanning a page and converting the resulting picture into text on the computer can be a 'hit or miss' process. The two key factors are the scanner itself and the software that interprets the picture into text.

1.5.2 *Scanning text*

The objective of scanning is to obtain an image of the printed words, and there are two obvious ways of doing this – hand-held scanner and flatbed scanner – and one less obvious method – fax.

Hand-held scanner
A hand-held scanner will scan a strip of about 4″ wide at a time. If this is done down the length of a page then you will probably need two strips to be joined together by the software – usually without much success.

!

▲ If you must use a hand-held scanner, set up the software to work in strips across the page and then use the OCR on each horizontal strip in turn.

▲ When using a hand-held scanner, place a wooden or plastic ruler to the side of the scanner to act as a guide; this will help ensure a straight scan.

▲ Have the scanner and software set for black and white (rather than colour or shades of grey) as this will give a crisper image for the OCR software to work with. Most scanners have various resolutions (dots per inch), and for text you should choose 200 or 300 dpi. The higher the resolution the greater the size of the final image and the bigger the file that you will need to work with.

Flatbed scanner
With a flatbed scanner, you can scan a complete A4 page in one go. The more sophisticated machines have sheet-feeders holding up to about 25 pages, and also optional accessories for transparencies, etc. However, this type of scanner will cost between five and ten times as much as a hand-held version. For example, using a flatbed scanner, a 90-page thesis originally typed manually can be scanned and converted into a word processor file in under three hours. The accuracy level will be high and the file will retain the original formatting, including paragraphs, and bold or italic characters.

Fax
If you do not have access to a scanner, then try fax technology. There are cheap fax-modems available which will allow a PC to send and receive fax messages, and the process that produces the image is precisely the same as that produced by a scanner.

Because of this, a number of fax-modems come with OCR software so that you can convert incoming faxes to text files you may edit. If you have access to one of these, by taking your document to the local fax machine and sending it to the PC by fax-modem and OCR software, you will have used the fax machine as a scanner.

1.5.3 Optical character recognition (OCR)

The process of taking the scanned image, which may be in PCX, TIFF, BMP or any other graphic format, and converting it to useable text is called optical character recognition. In essence, the software identifies lines of text and then attempts to identify each character in turn. A combination of quality of the image and sophistication of the software will determine whether, for example, a lower case 'L' is different from an upper case 'I'. This will depend on the quality of the image and the font (typeface) of the original, since there may be little difference – as this selection illustrates:

Font	Lower case 'L'	Upper case 'I'
Arial	l	I
Times Roman	l	I
Courier	l	I
Bookman	l	I

There are similar problems to be overcome with 0 (zero) and O (capital O). It is at this point that the result you achieve will depend on the sophistication of the OCR software, which will try to convert characters according to the context of the word and the contents of its built-in dictionary. For example, in 'will' the double 'L' at the end is part of a word to be found in the dictionary, while in '11.20' the double '1' is part of a numerical sequence. The more sophisticated the software, the greater the number of rules and tests it will attempt to apply.

Preparing for OCR
There are a number of hints that will help to improve the outcome. Try half a page first to see how successful the result is. If your test contains lots of ~~ (tilde) characters (which indicate failure to make sense of the text) you can try to improve the quality.

▲ Has the scanner been set to 300 dpi in black and white?

▲ Does the 'preview' image show clear, well defined characters? If not, try adjusting the scanner's brightness and contrast settings.

▲ Is the page 'square' in the scanner? If not, the 'preview' image will slope up or down the screen – it is usually better to re-scan rather than use the software to 'square' the image.

▲ Does the original have good contrast? An old faded document can often be improved by photocopying it first with a high contrast setting.

▲ Can the OCR software be set to recognize different font styles and sizes? There are normally only three choices of font: serif, sans-serif and dot matrix.

▲ Use correction fluid to remove 'noise' (such as marks or notes on the side) from the original document – then photocopy the page.

▲ Blank out diagrams with plain paper.

If, after you have tried all the above, your text appears as garbage, you may have no option than to have the document re-typed.

As yet, OCR software is unable to make sense of hand-written text, but that will change as the computer systems become more powerful and as more sophisticated software becomes available.

Post-OCR process
On completion of the OCR process, you will have an ASCII text file that will probably contain errors. Most OCR software will highlight unresolved characters at the end of the process, and give you the opportunity to edit them before saving the result to a file. This is fine for short documents on a fast machine, but you may have a 20-page document which you have left to run through an automatic sheet feeder. This will leave you a large number of unidentified characters to sort out in the document – you can choose the symbol to replace unrecognized characters – usually ~, # or @.

▲ Use the search facility on the word processor to locate unidentified characters which you can then correct.

▲ If a pattern of errors emerges, for example 'far' becoming 'for', you can use 'search and replace' throughout the document (but remember to check each change rather than risk introducing other mistakes).

▲ Use a spelling checker to pick up other errors.

▲ Proofread carefully, especially if there are numeric characters.

1.5.4 *Scanning graphical images*

Here again, the first question to ask yourself is whether you need to create a new image or transfer an existing one into electronic form.

▲ Do you need to store it in a digital format – possibly as part of a multimedia presentation?

▲ Will you want to transmit it electronically, possibly across a network?

▲ Do you have to perform some form of digital processing on it?

▲ Is the graphic to be included as part of a document or documents?

If you only need to include it once in a desktop published document, using a photocopier with enlarge/reduce facilities and a simple 'cut and paste' may well be a more cost-effective solution.

In this section the various types of image have been considered and the ways in which they may be 'digitized' will be covered in the following sections.

When you are considering how best to transfer an existing image from paper, a number of issues will affect your choice of method:

▲ physical size and format (ie whether black and white or colour, photograph or slide, etc) of the original

▲ output required – screen image or hard copy

▲ whether you need a colour or black and white image

▲ whether the capacity of your system will restrict the size of the stored file.

You also need to make sure that you will not be infringing copyright by reproducing the image.

Technology in Teaching   1.3   Copyright and intellectual property rights

Hand-held scanners

These are the cheapest of the digitizing options, and provide excellent results as long as you realise their limitations.

▲ Narrow scan width – typically 4″ – but with variable scan length.

▲ You need a steady hand to move the scanner over the image.

▲ May offer up to 400 dpi (dots per inch) resolution in 16, 32 or 256 shades of grey. Some offer colour scanning but quality varies, and a very slow and steady hand is required!

▲ Often come with some form of image editing (painting) software.

▲ Can establish links with existing DTP software to enable you to scan an image while working on a document.

Given the above limitations, the hand-held scanner offers an ideal way of digitizing small images and is especially successful when scanning drawings and images which involve few shades.

Flatbed scanners

These offer the greatest versatility and functionality, but are more expensive than the hand-held variety. An A4 flatbed scanner offering colour, scanning resolutions up to 1200 dpi, OCR and with sheet feed/transparency options may cost ten times as much as a hand-held scanner. If you are thinking of buying one, does the volume of work warrant the expense?

▲ File size can be huge! Choose the scanning format carefully – try to avoid 24-bit true colour modes at 600 dpi unless you really must have that degree of quality or

unless it is for only a small area of the picture. An A4 image may require up to 10Mb of storage at this colour and resolution setting and can slow the fastest of computers to a crawl.

▲ If the image is going to be viewed 'on screen', start at a low resolution and see what the image looks like – consider whether or not the system on which the final image will be viewed can support more than 256 colours.

1.5.5 *Digital photographs on CD (Photo-CD)*

This is a service available through a number of high street photographic developers and printers. The picture is digitized at source when the film is processed and the image stored on a special writeable CD. With the appropriate software, the image may then be read in any standard CD-drive, and an image of the desired resolution and colour depth extracted from the CD. This offers a number of advantages:

▲ very high image quality (as good as the camera used to create it) and most graphics packages will accept PCD (Photo-CD) images directly

▲ selectable resolution and colour depth – important when considering file sizes if the image is to be transferred over a network or put onto disk

▲ can transfer complete rolls of film (at processing time), and slides, negatives, even existing pictures can be added individually or in sets

▲ additional pictures can be added to the CD as required (up to 100 images)

▲ no need for expensive scanning equipment.

Set against this are the following disadvantages:

▲ it is relatively cheap to process and print one roll of 36-exposure film and put images onto Photo-CD (this includes the initial cost of the CD); having single images transferred is more expensive

▲ time – unlike the immediate results you get from electronic capture devices, you may have to wait a week before seeing the results

▲ preview and sequence is not possible with a roll of film: the pictures you take will go onto the CD – even the out-of-focus ones.

1.5.6 *Electronic image capture*

An alternative approach, especially where photographic images are to be used, is to consider capturing them in a digital form in the first instance. This avoids the need for processing film but at some cost to image quality.

Electronic cameras
Instead of digitizing an existing photograph, you take the picture electronically and then transfer the image into the PC. This is the principle behind still video cameras such as the Canon Ion. The unit itself functions in the same way as any other 'point and click' camera except that images are stored on a small, removable floppy disk.

This offers a number of advantages:

▲ no film has to be processed – you can display the results immediately on a domestic television or on a computer with a video capture card

▲ each disk will hold up to 50 images and may be re-used or kept as an archive; you can re-use individual frames at any time

▲ compact, built-in flash and possible macro facility

▲ direct transfer to a computer through optional disk reader or video capture card

▲ battery powered, it is ideal for field trips, etc.

The major drawbacks are the fairly low resolution of the image when compared with a scanner-produced image, the simple optics and the cost (which is about the same as a scanner).

Electronic camera backs

These are relatively few and far between, but allow the existing film capability of some of the more expensive cameras to be replaced by an electronic sensor that will provide the same facilities as the electronic camera, with the added advantage that all the existing lenses will be available. The major drawback is the cost both of the initial camera and the additional electronic 'back'.

Camcorders

The camcorder can offer the same facility as an electronic camera provided it has a single frame option. This will allow many hundreds of images to be captured onto video tape but, once again, image quality will not be great.

1.5.7 Video capture and playback

This is the final phase of the process and involves taking the video signal out from the source (camera, camcorder, videotape, etc) and capturing the signal in the computer. The process is specific to the video capture board and the software that uses it, but there are a few basic guidelines which apply to any system:

▲ Set the screen mode (colours and resolution) to one that reflects the way in which the final image will be used, but remember that more colours and higher resolution will mean a larger file.

▲ If the video source has options for SVHS (Super VHS) output and the capture card supports it, this will provide a higher quality image than using the UHF modulated output.

▲ Use high quality cables (gold plated plugs and properly shielded cable) to ensure that any 'noise' the computer generates does not affect the signal.

Digital video is developing rapidly. Until recently the options were AVI (Audio Video Interleaf) from Microsoft and QuickTime from Apple. Both these standards allow desktop computers to display video in a small window on the screen. More recently a new standard has appeared which allows the computer to display VHS quality, full screen video and sound.

MPEG (Motion Picture Expert Group) defines two methods for encoding digital video and is rapidly becoming the format of choice.

Video capture for AVI and QuickTime

With more and more emphasis being placed on multimedia applications, there is a growing demand for video clips to be included in applications. Such clips can greatly enhance the end result, but should not be undertaken without considering the potential difficulties.

Basic equipment

Video capture requires more hardware than perhaps any other computer-based activity. For AVI and QuickTime movies the practical minimum is:

▲ powerful computer (486 processor minimum for a PC)

▲ large memory (at least 8Mb)

▲ large hard disk (10–15Mb free for each minute of captured video)

▲ video capture card such as Videoblaster or VideoLogic (plus software, which is usually supplied with the card); if you are using Windows, check that the card will work with your version of Windows and video card

▲ video source (video camera and/or video recorder).

A few video capture cards will not capture sound, so you will need a separate audio card. It is possible to get video capture cards that compress the data in real time before writing the data to the disk. These cards are far more expensive than those employing post-capture compression.

Troubleshooting

Most problems are caused through incorrect cabling and software set-up, so if your video source fails to display or is incorrect, on a PC check:

▲ that the output from the SVGA is fed into the video capture card, and that the monitor is connected to the correct output on the capture card

▲ that the internal linking cable from the video capture card to the SVGA card is correctly installed

▲ that the screen resolution and colour depth being used by Windows is suitable for your video capture software

▲ that the correct 'video source' is selected in the capture software

▲ that the cables from the source to the capture card are correct

▲ that there is enough space on your hard disk

▲ that 'preview mode' in the software is available and switched on

▲ if colours look 'odd', that the software is set to the correct input source (usually PAL or SVHS, but not NTSC).

If all else fails, then connect the source to a television to check that there is a signal coming out of the source in the first place.

At the end of the process, you should end up with a video clip that displays in colour, with sound, in about a quarter of the screen and requiring about 10Mb of storage for each minute of video.

Video capture: MPEG

MPEG is a compression standard for digital video, which comes in two levels: level 1 and level 2. It allows desktop computers to display VHS-quality video and audio from networks, CD-ROM or local hard drives. Level 2 is a professional standard requiring very expensive equipment.

To be displayed at its best, MPEG requires a display adapter such as the Videoblaster. There are software viewers available from ftp sources on the Internet but these viewers need a fast machine to give any kind of useful output. Most modern cards will display MPEG, AVI, CDi and QuickTime as well as being able to encode the older AVI-type video.

Real time encoding can be acheived using an MPEG card in a PC. The standard will allow different data rates, so it is important to use one which is compatible with the network, CD-ROM or hard disk used for output. Too much data per second will cause the display to halt to catch up – too little and the quality of the video will suffer. Video on demand will probably use one of the MPEG standards, so its take-up is pretty much assured.

1.6   *Presenting your information in a lecture theatre*

Once you have got information into the computer, you will need to find ways of presenting this material. If it is in the form of a computer learning package or a computer-based presentation, the computer itself will be the presentation medium. You may also need to produce notes or OHP acetate slides for a presentation.

Here are the most usual methods of using material stored on a computer which you want to present to a group in a lecture theatre:

▲ an overhead projector (OHP) with acetates

▲ an OHP with a display panel

▲ an 'active' projector

▲ a large television screen

Each of the last three requires some form of presentation software such as Microsoft PowerPoint, Harvard Graphics, Aldus Persuasion or WordPerfect Presentations. Presentation systems make it easy for you to produce multimedia presentations of 'slides' incorporating text, audio, video clips and spreadsheet information. In addition to offering multimedia facilities, these packages enable you to create professional-looking presentations with:

▲ initial editing of the text into frames

▲ graphic images where required

▲ changing from one image to the next, either by time or by key-press

▲ partial reveal of a frame

▲ links to graphing and charting software

▲ a variety of fades and wipes from one image to the next

▲ the facility to re-order the sequence

▲ slide design to give your slides a consistent, professional look

▲ various fades and wipes between slides for smooth delivery.

Once you have created your 'slides' or screens of information, you will be able to present this information. Some of the equipment available to do this is described briefly here.

1.6.1 *Overhead projector (OHP)*

An OHP enables you to project acetate foils onto a large screen. Foils or 'transparencies' can be produced from word-processed documents, graphics, spreadsheet or presentation software. In fact, anything that can be printed onto paper from the computer can be printed onto acetates for OHPs.

1.6.2 *Liquid crystal display (LCD) panel*

A piece of equipment placed on the overhead projector, a display panel replaces the transparency itself with a LCD about 25cm square. The panel itself is connected to your computer so that information on your computer can be viewed via the larger OHP screen. The resolution and number of colours the panel provides can vary greatly and the panels are less well suited to moving images.

!

▲ When giving your presentation, you need either to take your own portable computer and connect it to the LCD panel, or to use a floppy disk of your material on a 'resident' computer system.

▲ The projector has to be a bright (400w) high-quality unit.

▲ It is essential to keep the ambient lighting quite low (if you cannot darken the room do not use an LCD panel: you would do better to use OHP transparencies).

▲ If in doubt, take OHP transparencies as well.

1.6.3 'Active' projector

The active projector offers the highest quality output to a large screen. Typically, a ceiling-mounted Barco unit can display a video or computer image on a three-metre screen. Similar technology has now been developed for portable units which can be taken into any lecture theatre or seminar room. Most will work with a range of computer equipment, so whether you use PC or Mac you should have no compatibility problems.

▲ Make sure that the correct cables are available

▲ Check that the unit will work at the display resolution you wish to use (if the resolution is not right, you may get an unstable or flickering image).

1.6.4 TV modulator

A TV modulator allows a computer to be used with a domestic television receiver by taking the monitor output and converting it into a UHF (TV) signal. The quality of the resulting image may be poor, but the units are relatively inexpensive.

1.7 Producing acetates

The simplest method is to photocopy onto acetate. Alternatively, a laser printer can print directly onto acetate. You can make colour acetates by using a colour photocopier or printing from a colour laser printer.

Use the correct type of acetate sheet for a photocopier or laser printer: an ordinary acetate sheet melting on contact with the hot drum may cause permanent damage!

Inkjet printers can print directly onto special matt-finish acetate but because of the surface you cannot remove additional jottings. Colour inkjet printers are cheaper and more readily available than colour laser printers (although the acetates you have to use with inkjets are more expensive than the laser-compatible ones).

Inkjet printers require a different type of acetate from the normal sheets for use with an OHP pen and those used for laser printers and photocopiers. You are unlikely to damage the printer by using the wrong type, but your acetate will be a mess and you will have wasted ink!

Technology in Teaching   1.8.3   Presentation software

1.8 Making a presentation using a computer

Giving a presentation using an LCD-panel or projector requires far more expertise and confidence in the equipment than simply using a set of prepared transparencies. As with any high-tech method, the end result will probably either be far more impressive than the more workaday OHP presentation – or an absolute disaster if things go wrong. Careful planning, preparation and practice are vital!

1.8.1 What do you need?

▲ Software to create and manage the sequence.

▲ Material to present as a 'slide show'.

▲ A computer in the location or a portable you can take with you.

▲ Either an OHP + LCD panel or an active projection unit.

▲ A plan for coping if the above fails in some way!

1.8.2 Creating your presentation

Begin by assembling your material in computer-readable (digital) format. You can use material from a spreadsheet, scanned text or pictures, sound and video clips. You can use this material within the presentation software along with any text you want to add. The sequence of the presentation can then be tried out.

1.8.3 Presentation software

With presentation software you can produce links between the frames, with fancy wipes and fades from one frame to the next, uncover 'hidden' frames, and create a consistent style through a sequence.

One feature of most software of this type is the facility to 'tile' four slides and produce a hard copy. This allows you to provide printed copies of your acetates and with four slides on each page you can achieve considerable savings in terms of reprographics.

When making your presentation, if you have to rely on a computer system that is not the one on which the material was developed, then:

▲ ensure that the software you need is available on the machine you intend to use

▲ check that the machine is capable of using the screen resolution for which you prepared your slides

▲ above all – check it out first!

Using Technology   2.3   Harnessing new technology

Warren (1994) *Understanding IT: computer-based presentations*[1]
Riley (1993) *Computer-based presentations: a demonstration package*[2]

Besides producing computer-driven presentations, presentation software can also produce acetates for overhead projectors, which will give your slides a more professional look than ones you have written, drawn or even photocopied from typescript – although, of course, this reduces your media to text and pictures. These are the most widely used presentation media in lecture theatres everywhere – quite simply because of the ease of production, simplicity and robustness. The following tips can help when producing acetates (sometimes called 'foils', 'slides' or 'transparencies'):

▲ use a suitable point size (size of print): if text is readable with the naked eye at two metres, visibility should be fine

▲ use a clear font (style of print); generally sans serif fonts such as Helvetica are easier to read from a distance than serif fonts such as Times

▲ aim to have no more than five main bullet points per frame

▲ avoid complex tables – try using a chart instead

▲ keep a consistent style: choose a border (frame) style and use it throughout the series

▲ numbering your slides saves problems when trying to order them!

1.8.4 *Using an LCD panel*

LCD panels offer a means of projecting a computer image onto a screen, using an OHP as the light source, with an LCD panel that may be used alongside or may replace the display screen. This panel is laid on top of the projector and takes the place of acetates.

Connect the panel to the computer by plugging the cable into the connector where the monitor would normally go, and then plug the monitor into an output socket on the panel. The panel will also need a power supply and an OHP with a bright bulb – typically 400 watts.

▲ Create the slides as if you were going to print them out.

▲ Make copies of the sequence on acetate unless you are very confident!

▲ For clarity, avoid coloured text on coloured backgrounds.

▲ Switch off the OHP light when not showing a slide, as some LCD units begin to fade if they get too warm.

▲ Bear in mind that moving images often look 'fuzzy' because of the slow refresh rate of liquid crystal.

▲ To minimize potential problems try to take along your own computer – especially if you have access to a portable.

▲ If you must use a machine other than your own, check it for viruses first, or check your floppy disk before using it again in your computer.

Technology in Teaching   1.12   Computer viruses

1.8.5 *Using an LCD projector*

These combine both projector and panel into a single unit that may be regarded as 'portable'. As with an LCD panel, the projector plugs into the monitor output of the computer, and the monitor plugs into the projector. Setting up is quite straightforward, projection quality is usually better than with a panel and there are fewer things to go wrong. However, the cost is higher than for an LCD panel and OHP projector.

Using Technology   2.3.1   Using technology to make lecture material a flexible resource

1.8.6 *Using an active projector*

Active projectors, such as Barco, are projectors which are usually fixed permanently to the ceiling or floor, with connections to the point where the computer or video source is located. You can treat them in just the same way as the LCD projector, and they will produce a good image up to three metres wide.

1.8.7 *General points about display*

A number of points apply, irrespective of the display method you have selected:

▲ try to use subdued lighting – avoid bright sunlight at all costs

▲ use a projection screen rather than a wall (the reflective metallised surface will give better image quality)

▲ ensure that the systems optics are clean before you start

▲ make sure the image remains in focus

▲ avoid trailing cables: you or others may trip over them.

1.9   Producing hard copies

How you print out your work depends on the type of hard copy you require and the budget available. The first choice is whether or not you need to print in colour. Once that decision is made, the type of printing technology needs to be considered: each has its own advantages and disadvantages.

!

When buying a printer, take into account the following:
- ▲ whether to have colour or black and white
- ▲ print quality (can it produce half-tones for photographic images?)
- ▲ cost of printing per page – including all the consumables
- ▲ whether or not it is PostScript compatible (fast, industry-standard)
- ▲ size of built-in memory to allow large graphic images to be printed (at least 2Mb)
- ▲ time taken to print a page
- ▲ initial purchase cost
- ▲ ongoing running, repair and maintenance costs
- ▲ noise level.

The sections which follow outline some points to bear in mind when selecting a printer.

1.9.1   Dot matrix printer

Dot matrix printers work by using a number of pins, usually nine or 24, to build up each character as a series of dots as the print head moves across the paper: the more pins, the finer the image.

Advantages
- ▲ Cheap
- ▲ Reliable
- ▲ Use either fan-fold (continuous) stationery or single A4 sheets.

Disadvantages
- ▲ Slow
- ▲ Little built-in memory as a print buffer
- ▲ Noisy
- ▲ Low print quality
- ▲ Colour available on some but quality poor compared to inkjets.

1.9.2 Inkjet (bubblejet) printer

These work by projecting tiny droplets of ink at the paper from either a black or three-colour cartridge. Some colour inkjet printers create black by using all three of the colours, while others have separate black and colour cartridges. The print quality can be high, especially if you use the correct paper. You can usually print directly onto OHP transparencies, but it is essential to use only the special inkjet-compatible acetates (which tend to be expensive).

Advantages
▲ Good print quality, even on low-cost photocopier paper
▲ Colour available (quality good on special paper)
▲ Quiet in operation
▲ Accept A4 paper, usually into a 50–100 sheet feeder
▲ Will print halftone images
▲ Print directly onto acetate (but check you have the right sort).

Disadvantages
▲ Ink will run if made wet
▲ Ink cartridges are expensive (especially those that include a new print head to maintain quality)
▲ Special inkjet paper and OHP transparencies are expensive
▲ Not all will accept cheap continuous stationery.

! You will see kits advertised for refilling ink cartridges. Do not be tempted by them! Filling cartridges is a messy and potentially (for the printer) dangerous process. If refill ink clogs a print head you may have to call out someone to put it right. It may be less of a problem with cartridges which include the print head (as in Hewlett-Packard printers) but there is still the possibility of ink draining from the refilled cartridge and damaging the electronics – especially with portables. For the sake of a few pounds it is hardly worth the risk.

1.9.3   *Laser and LED printers*

These work on the same principle as photocopiers: that is, an image of the page is created and transferred (by laser or light-emitting diode) to a sensitised drum in the printer. Toner (black or coloured powder) is then attracted to the drum according to where the drum has been illuminated, and the toner transferred to the paper and fixed by heat.

Advantages
▲ High quality, can be better than 600 dpi
▲ Fast – some print up to 12 or 16 ppm (pages per minute)
▲ Good half-tone capability
▲ PostScript available
▲ Quiet in operation
▲ Multiple bin options (i.e. more than one paper source).

Disadvantages
▲ Purchase price higher than for inkjet or dot matrix
▲ Consumables (toner cartridges) expensive
▲ A3 and colour laser printers are available but still very expensive.

1.9.4   *Colour laser printer*

Working on the same principle as a monochrome laser, the colour laser can produce excellent print quality. The major drawback is the initial cost which, at present, is six to ten times that of a black laser printer. As with all computer technology, however, the cost will fall in the next few years.

1.9.5 *Combined fax/scanner/copier/printer*

One fairly recent development is that of a combined fax/scanner/copier/printer in one unit. Since many of the functions are common to more than one process it makes sense to combine them all in a single unit. One drawback is the relatively low scan resolution of 200 dpi, but this will be adequate unless scan quality is a top priority for you.

1.10 *Backing up your files*

It is one of life's certainties that at some time or other your computer will go wrong. If the hard disk 'crashes' – a term used to describe terminal failure – you will lose all the data that was on the disk. It may be possible to have it repaired by sending it to a specialist recovery firm, but this is an expensive option and not guaranteed to be 100% successful. (If your computer 'hangs' or 'locks up', it may be because of a temporary software problem, so switch off or reboot: if the cause is not fatal, you will have lost just the data you have entered since you last saved any of your open files.)

Now since you will have all the original software disks, the operating system and applications can be restored quite quickly once the system has been repaired. What cannot be replaced are the files you have created using the software – that is, unless you have taken a few basic precautions:

▲ Keep at least one copy of every one of your working files on floppy disk at all times.

▲ Use sensible names for your files and make good use of directory structures.

▲ If using a personal area on a network file server, find out how and when the system is backed up.

There are two main factors to consider when backing up files:

▲ Will the file(s) fit on a single floppy disk or small number of disks?

▲ How easy will it be for you to use the backed-up copy if you need to?

1.10.1 *Floppy disks*

Most computers use the 3.5″ high-density disks which provide 1.44Mb of storage: this is enough for more than 250 pages of A4 text. However, a scanned image may require 2Mb or more, so a single floppy disk would be unable to hold the data, and a 5-minute video clip, at 50Mb, would present even more problems.

Back-up software
In order to get round this limitation, most back-up software (such as that supplied

with Windows) will split the file or files over a number of floppy disks and compress the data at the same time in order to minimise the storage space needed. The same software will enable you to back up your entire hard disk, but for a full back-up a 540Mb hard disk with 30% compression would require more than 250 floppy disks, each taking at least a minute to be written!

To avoid damaging a computer system, it is important to take proper care of floppy disks and not leave them on parcel shelves in cars, where they are likely to develop wrinkles, or use them as coffee mats, drop them in puddles, or sit on them. Provided the magnetic media (the thin circle inside the disk case) has not been destroyed, it is often possible to open the plastic casing and transfer the disk into the plastic case of another. Don't bother trying to reassemble the shutter mechanism (which is very fiddly to do), since once you have managed to get any data off the disk you will need to throw it away.

If the disk is very dirty or sticky, wash it gently with soapy water and make sure you dry it thoroughly. You may be surprised at how much data you can recover and, after all, you have nothing to lose by trying to clean up your disk.

1.10.2 *Spare hard disks*

With the price of computer hardware constantly falling, one option is to add an extra hard disk drive. You can connect the second one to your computer externally through the parallel printer port, which has the advantage that a number of machines may use the disk drive.

1.10.3 *Tape streamers*

Developments in data compression mean that it is now possible to back up 850Mb on a single low-cost tape. At about 10Mb per minute, the data transfer rate is relatively slow, but there are advantages in being able to store data on a removable medium, so that each month or each week you can put your work on a separate tape from which individual files may be extracted. At present an 850Mb tape streamer and a hard disk cost about the same.

1.10.4 *DAT tapes*

Digital tape technology offers storage capacities of 2Gb (2000Mb) or more on a single tape with a very fast (50Mb per minute) back-up speed. This makes them ideal for file servers where a daily back-up and a fast recovery rate are necessary. The major drawback is the cost: a 4Gb DAT drive currently costs four times as much as a 1Gb hard disk drive.

1.10.5 Flopticals

New developments in disk technology have meant that it is now possible to store 200Mb on a 3.5" floppy disk – but not the same ones that we normally use. The new drives, however, read and write ordinary 3.5" floppy disks as well as the 200Mb disks.

1.10.6 Writeable CD-ROMs

With the reduction in cost of both the recorders and the media itself, it is now possible to use CD-ROMs for back-up purposes. This only makes sense if you have finalized the work, since once the file is written to CD-ROM it cannot be altered or deleted; you would have to save a complete newer version on the disc.

1.10.7 Network back-ups

If you are working in a networked environment, your file area is backed up regularly with the contents of the file server. This may be worth checking before going to the bother and expense of adding back-up hardware to your own system. If a copy of your work is needed elsewhere, away from the network, however, you will need to make a copy on removable media. Alternatively, it might be possible to get the destination machine onto the network (perhaps via the Internet) to transfer the file that way.

1.10.8 Other methods

Disk drives that connect to the parallel port, and are therefore transferable from machine to machine, are growing in popularity. These portable disk drives use their own disks and offer a storage capacity in excess of 100Mb.

You may have heard of storing computer data on a domestic video recorder – this has been tried but has not really been a success.

1.10.9 Back-up method comparison chart

Device	Maximum capacity	Cost of drive	Cost of media	Speed*	Removable media
Floppy disk	2.88 Mb	Low	Low	Slow	Yes
Additional hard disk	Cost and capacity as system			Same	No
Tape streamer	1000 Mb	<$340	<$510	Medium	Yes
DAT tape	8000 Mb	<$850	<$34	Fast	Yes
Floptical	200 Mb	<$680	<$51	Medium	Yes
Writeable CD	650 Mb	<$850	<$34	Fast	Yes
Network				Fast	N/A
Zip drive	100 Mb	<$340	<$34	Medium	Yes
Removable hard disk	Cost and capacity as system			Same	Yes

* Speed compared to the existing hard disk drive

1.11 Keeping data safe

Having spent many hours producing a document or application, how can you minimize the chance of losing it all? How can you prevent unauthorized users from accessing it?

Start by considering some of the things that could go wrong:

▲ catastrophic system failure such as a hard disk crash

▲ accidental deletion or overwriting

▲ deliberate deletion

▲ file corruption through system failure

▲ file corruption through virus infection

▲ loss of the computer through fire or theft.

1.11.1 Back-up procedures

You can recover from most, if not all, of these – provided you have taken adequate back-up measures. This usually entails maintaining three copies of a file and saving each new generation of the file on a new disk, so that if a problem appears there are three previous versions available to go back to. If the cause of the problem is identified as a virus, then either it can be removed or you can use an earlier, uninfected version of your file.

1.11.2 Preventing unauthorized access

If others have access to your computer system it is almost impossible to stop files being deleted or copied. One precaution is to make the file 'password protected' – this will ensure that you are the only person with access to the file. Others may try to access it, but the contents will be scrambled until the correct password is given. This does not prevent the file being deleted or stop someone from reformatting your hard disk, but it does offer one further level of security.

1.12 Computer viruses

If you are not connected to a network and use no floppy disks other than your own and stick with original (write-protected) master disks, then the chances of getting a virus are nil. If you regularly swap disks with others, 'borrow' software or belong to an electronic bulletin board system (BBS) then the chances are that at some time your system will be hit by a virus.

1.12.1 What is a virus?

A definition of computer viruses is: 'A program that modifies other programs by placing a copy of itself inside them.' This definition is somewhat simplified, and does not cover all virus types, but is sufficient to show the major difference between viruses and so-called 'Trojan' programs, which is that the virus replicates, but the Trojan does not. A Trojan is a program that pretends to do something useful (or at least interesting), but when run, it may have some harmful effect such as scrambling your FAT (File Allocation Table) or formatting the hard disk.

Both viruses and Trojans may contain a 'time-bomb', intended to destroy programs or data on a specific date or when some condition has been fulfilled. A time bomb is often designed to be harmful, maybe doing something like formatting the hard disk, but sometimes it is relatively harmless, perhaps slowing the computer down every Friday or making a ball bounce around the screen.

However, there is really no such thing as a harmless virus. Even if a virus has been intended to cause no damage, it may still do so in certain cases – often because of the incompetence of the virus writer. A fairly innocuous virus may be modified, either by the original author or by someone else, so that a more harmful version of it appears. It is also possible that the modification produces a less harmful virus, but that has only rarely happened.

The damage caused by a virus may consist of the deletion of data or programs, maybe even reformatting of the hard disk, but more subtle damage is also possible. Some viruses may modify data or introduce typing errors into text, while other viruses may not be intended to do anything other than just replicating.

Most viruses try to recognize existing infections, so they do not infect what has already been infected. This makes it possible to 'inoculate' against specific viruses by making the 'victim' appear to be infected. However, this method is ineffective as a general defence, as it is not possible to inoculate the same program against multiple viruses.

In general, viruses are rather unusual programs, often simple, and written just like any other program. It does not take a genius to write one – any average assembly language programmer can easily do it, but fortunately few of them do.

1.12.2 Common misconceptions about viruses

▲ A virus cannot spread from one type of computer to another. For example, a virus designed to infect Macintosh computers cannot infect PCs and vice versa.

▲ A virus cannot appear all by itself: it has to be written, just like any other program. Not all viruses are harmful; some may only cause minor damage as a side effect.

▲ A virus cannot infect a computer unless it is booted from an infected disk or unless you run an infected program on it. Merely reading data from an infected disk cannot cause an infection.

▲ A write-protected disk cannot become infected.

▲ A virus cannot attach itself to data files, so viruses cannot be distributed with them.

1.12.3 How do you avoid getting a computer virus?

There are a number of packages for both PCs and Macs that will provide protection against viruses, but you can also take some simple precautions of your own.

▲ Rule number one is *make back-ups.*Keep good back-up copies (more than one) of everything you really do not want to lose. This will not only protect you from serious damage caused by viruses, but is also necessary in case of hardware failure.

▲ Never boot a computer with a hard disk from a floppy disk.

▲ If the computer has no hard disk, but is booted from a disk, always use the same disk, and keep it write-protected.

▲ Keep all disks write-protected unless you need to write to them. When you obtain new software on a disk, write-protect the disk before making a back-up copy of it.

▲ Be really careful about your sources of software. In general, shrink-wrapped commercial software should be 'clean', but there have been a few documented cases of infected commercial software. Public domain, freeware and shareware packages do not have to be any more dangerous than commercial ones – it all depends on the source. If you obtain software from a BBS, check what precautions the sysop (system operator – the person running the BBS) takes against viruses. If he does not screen the software made available for downloading, you should find another source.

▲ Check all new software for infection before you run it for the first time. It is even advisable to use a couple of scanners from different manufacturers, as no single scanner is able to detect all viruses.

1.12.4 *How do you know if your computer has a virus?*

Look out for any unusual behaviour on your computer:

▲ Does it take longer than usual to load programs?

▲ Do unusual error messages appear?

▲ Does the memory size seem to have decreased?

▲ Do the disk lights stay on longer than they used to?

▲ Do files just disappear?

Anything like this may indicate a virus infection. If your computer is infected with a virus, don't panic! Sometimes a badly thought-out attempt to remove a virus will do much more damage than the virus itself would. If you are not sure what to do, leave your computer turned off until you find someone who knows how to remove the virus safely.

Remember that some viruses may interfere with the disinfecting operation if they are active in memory at that time, so before attempting to disinfect you MUST boot the computer from a clean system disk.

It is also a good idea to boot from a clean system disk before scanning for viruses, as several 'stealth' viruses are extremely difficult to detect if they are active in memory during virus scanning.

References for Chapter 1

[1] Warren, Lorraine (1994), *Understanding IT: computer-based presentations*, University of Hull, ITTI
Looks at choosing hardware and software for computer-based presentations as well as giving some information on design.
Order from UCoSDA, tel: 0114 272 5248 or email: ucosda@sheffield.ac.uk

[2] Riley, Fred (1993), *Computer-based presentations: a demonstration package*, University of Hull, ITTI
This is a floppy disk discussing what presentation packages are and general guidelines for use.
Contact Fred Riley at the University of Hull, tel: 01482 466316 or email: F.H.Riley@ucc.hull.ac.uk

2   How to get connected to the Internet

This chapter presents information about computer networks and how you can access them. Here is an overview of the main topics covered:

▲ computer networks: from the local area network (LAN) that links the PCs in your department to the Internet that links computers all around the world

▲ JANET: the UK academic network that links colleges and universities to each other and to the Internet

▲ the Internet: what it is, how it works, and an overview of the services it makes available

▲ getting connected: everything you need to know about the hardware, software and services needed to use the Internet.

2.1   *What is a computer network?*

At the most basic level, a computer network comprises two or more computers which are linked in order that they can exchange data. The computers are usually linked by electrical cables plugged into special communications ports. So that the computers on the network 'speak the same language', they must follow the same set of rules to control communications between them. The sets of rules are known as protocols.

2.1.1   *Stand-alone computers*

A stand-alone computer is one that is a complete system in itself and is not connected to other computers. It may have other devices attached to it, such as a scanner for input and a printer for output, but all the information available is stored locally, either on the hard disk or on removable media such as floppy disks or CD-ROMs.

2.1.2   *Computers on a local area network*

A local area network (LAN) is a way of connecting several computers in the same building to enable them to share hardware, software and data resources. Each computer on the network needs a special network card and communications software to allow it to send and receive data via the network cable. Some computers have the network card built in as standard.

If your PC is attached to a LAN, you can:

– send files and messages to other people on the LAN
– access databases and other files held centrally on a file server
– share the use of expensive devices such as laser printers.

The simplest arrangement of computers on a LAN is called peer-to-peer, in which all the computers on the LAN have equal status. Common operating systems such as

Microsoft Windows 95 and Apple's System 7 have simple built-in file-sharing features which allow users to access files held on the other computers. Users can also send each other messages and print to any printer attached to the LAN.

This type of network is often arranged as a daisy-chain (see below), and is only suitable for small networks with a maximum of (say) ten computers. The advantages of this arrangement are that it is easy and cheap to set up, but a disadvantage is that it is not very resilient – if someone unplugs their network cable, the whole network fails.

A daisy-chain network is a simple solution for a small number of computers.

A simple peer-to-peer daisy-chain network

A better solution is to use a backbone arrangement, where each computer is separately attached to a cable running in a duct. This allows computers to be unplugged without affecting the rest of the network.

Many local area networks (LANs) use a backbone to link computers, file servers and printers.

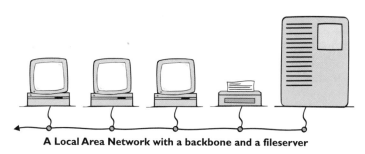

A Local Area Network with a backbone and a fileserver

The best solution is to use a star arrangement, although this requires a piece of hardware called a hub, which acts as the centre of the star. This arrangement is not only resilient but also improves the performance of the network, especially when large amounts of data need to be moved.

The star arrangement offers many advantages, but it involves extra costs for wiring and hardware.

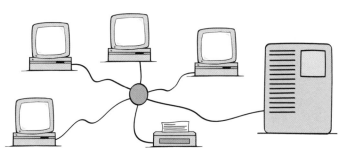

A Local Area Network with a star and a hub

There are several types of LAN technology, of which Ethernet is the most popular. Others include the IBM Token Ring and Apple's AppleTalk. There are also different types of cable, which vary in size, cost and reliability: the most popular is 10BaseT. Most LANs have a dedicated computer called a file server: this provides secure storage for files which can be accessed by all authorized users. The file server runs special network software (for example, Novell Netware) which handles all the operational requirements of the network, such as security, printer queues and reliable file-sharing. To run this type of network efficiently, you should have a network manager to administer it and ensure that everything runs smoothly. The network manager should regularly make copies of the files on the server using a tape back-up device so that important files can be recovered if anything goes wrong.

2.1.3 *Campus networks*

Many academic institutions are now investing in campus-wide networks. These link departmental LANs to central facilities such as high-performance computers and electronic mail servers. Some establishments have installed fibre-optic cables that act as a high-speed 'spine' within the network.

Campus networks provide a convenient and managed link to other academic and international networks such as JANET and the Internet. They also make it easy for departments to communicate with central administrative systems (such as management and administrative computing (MAC) initiative systems).

A campus-wide network. Note the fibre-optic spine linking the departmental LANs and central services, and the gateway router used to connect to the outside world.

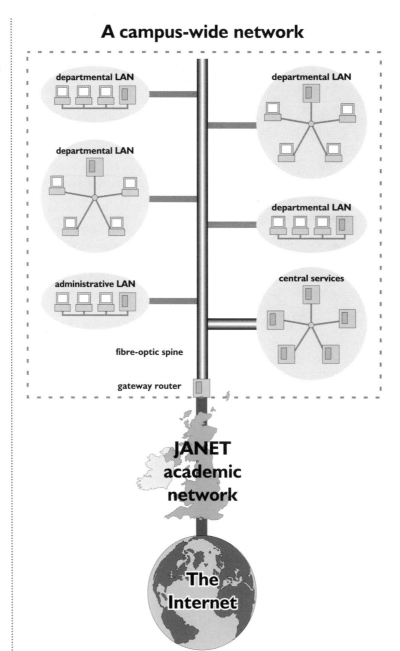

A campus-wide network

departmental LAN

departmental LAN

departmental LAN

departmental LAN

administrative LAN

central services

fibre-optic spine

gateway router

JANET academic network

The Internet

2.1.4 *National networks*

Networks which consist of linked LANs are known as WANs – wide area networks.

The Joint Academic NETwork (JANET) is a centrally funded network linking most universities in the UK. JANET allows them to share resources such as high-performance computers, data sets, software archives and information. It also facilitates communication between academics, administrators and other staff, encouraging collaboration and the sharing of experience and knowledge.

Some other nations have networks like JANET, but most rely on commercial networks to connect their academic institutions to the Internet. The institutions negotiate their own arrangements with network companies.

Technology in Teaching   2.2   JANET: the Joint Academic NETwork

2.1.5 *International networks*

There are many national and international academic networks, but the one everybody is talking about is the Internet. The Internet is a 'network of networks' which are unified by the communications protocol they use (known as TCP/IP) and the standardised addresses used by the computer systems.

Technology in Teaching   2.3   The Internet

2.1.6 *Commercial networks*

Commercial networks provide network services (including Internet access) for business and home users. You need a modem and a phone line to connect your PC with a commercial network. Special software is used to provide an easy-to-use interface to the services available. Payment for use of the services is usually made by credit card.

Technology in Teaching   2.4.3   Commercial Internet service providers (ISPs)

2.2   *JANET: the Joint Academic NETwork*

JANET is the UK academic and research network which links universities, colleges and research organizations throughout the UK. The network evolved from separate regional and national research networks and now forms part of the Internet.

The main things you will need to know about JANET are it

▲ offers free (centrally funded) Internet access to all connected institutions

▲ enables people within those institutions to communicate and collaborate using computers

▲ provides national access to services such as high-performance computers, data, document and software archives

▲ has a policy which defines acceptable uses and forbids non-educational use.

Further information about JANET is available from these Internet addresses:

Web address: *http://www.ukerna.ac.uk*
ftp address: *www.ukerna.ac.uk/pub/newsfiles/*

2.3 The Internet

You have almost certainly heard about the 'Internet' or 'Information Superhighway', but you can be forgiven if you are not sure what it really is. Here are some comments you may have come across in relation to the Internet:

– 'The Internet joins up computers all over the world.'
– 'You can discuss almost anything with other people on the Internet.'
– 'Hackers use the Internet to break into defence computers.'
– 'Children can easily find pornography on the Internet.'
– 'Finding what you need is like looking for a needle in a haystack.'

These comments all have some validity, but the Internet is so vast and amorphous that they do not really even begin to describe what it is and what it can be used for.

2.3.1 What is the Internet?

The Internet is a network of networks. By using a standard set of rules which define how computers communicate with each other, these networks are able to pass data freely from one side of the globe to the other. These 'rules' are a computer communications protocol called TCP/IP.

By March 1996 it was estimated that the Internet connected half a million computers and had 35 million users. The rate of growth in terms of users is estimated to be 10% per month.

The Internet only exists as an agreement between various computer networks. It is not centrally managed, funded or planned. The Internet Society is a voluntary organization which tries to ensure that the Internet evolves to meet the needs of its users, but the standards set by the Society cannot be enforced. The only reason that the Internet works is through the co-operation of all organizations and people who make up the Internet.

2.3.2 *How are computers identified on the Internet?*

Every computer on the Internet has a unique IP (Internet Protocol) address, written as four numbers (each less than 256) separated by dots. The IP address of the PC on my desk, for example, is 152.78.64.98.

Addresses are partly assigned by the Internet Network Information Centre to prevent duplication. The first two numbers represent a country, network and organization. The third and fourth numbers are assigned locally to individual networks and computers. At the current rate of growth, the Internet will have to extend its numbering scheme before the end of the century.

Because people do not find long numbers easy to remember, an equivalent system of names has been adopted. The format for Internet address names is machine.site.domain (see table below). My PC's Internet address can be expressed as *baldrick.ilc.soton.ac.uk*, where 'baldrick' is the name I chose for my PC, 'ilc' is the unit I work for (Interactive Learning Centre), 'soton' represents University of Southampton, 'ac' is the JANET academic network, and 'uk' is the United Kingdom.

machine	network & site	domain
baldrick	*.ilc.soton*	*.ac.uk*

The domain name gives you information about the nature and geographical location of the organisation; for example all higher education establishments in the UK which use JANET have the domain 'ac.uk'. All countries except the USA have a two-letter identifier – for example, 'uk' is the United Kingdom, 'de' is Germany, 'fr' is France.

Instead of the two-letter country identifier, the USA uses these domain names:

com	commercial organizations
edu	educational institutions
gov	governmental entities
int	international organizations
mil	US military
net	network resources
org	other organizations.

2.3.3 *What has the Internet to offer?*

The Internet basically offers two main facilities:
- a means of communication
- information.

You can communicate with individuals and groups using electronic mail (email). You

A full list of country codes can be found on the World Wide Web at http://devito.ssml.ed.ac.uk/www/country.html

can join mailing lists and news groups, which enable people to exchange views and information on almost any subject. The size of the Internet is so great that there are usually enough people to support discussions about any academic (or other) interest. Through mailing lists and news groups you can get expert help, advice and information at no cost – people like to be helpful! In turn, you should be willing to contribute your own expertise where relevant – co-operation means that everyone gains.

Some examples of mailing lists and news groups

airpollution-biology: A UK academic mailing list for groups wishing to discuss aspects of the biological/environmental impact of air pollution. Topics covered include biochemistry, physiology, ecology, genetics, and an understanding of the processes underlying the responses to air pollutants.

alt.hypnosis: An Internet Usenet group dedicated to aspects of hypnosis, in particular the merits of 'New Age' hypnosis tapes.

bionet.immunology: An Internet discussion group for biological scientists interested in immunology.

Technology in Teaching   4   Communicating using computers

You can access a wide range of information resources stored as files on the Internet. Resource indexes such as Archie, Veronica and Web databases use keyword searching to help you to find useful resources quickly. Software tools (such as ftp, Gopher and Mosaic) are available to enable you to view and retrieve files for local use. These resources are freely available – and if you have useful resources which you can make available on the Internet, so much the better for everyone.

Some typical information resources

HENSA, the Higher Education National Software Archive, is based at Lancaster University in the UK. This site has large archives of public domain software for most popular types of PC. A similar site at the University of Kent has an extensive collection of UNIX utilities, code and software.

AskERIC is an information service for educators, based at Syracuse University in the USA. ERIC is the Educational Resources Information Centre, a federally funded, national information system which offers a variety of services and products on a broad range of education-related issues.

The **BUBL Information Service** at the University of Strathclyde is funded as a national information service by JISC. It originated as the BUlletin Board for Libraries but now has a World Wide Web site which provides an information service to the UK academic and research community in general, with much of this taking place via the BUBL Subject Tree.

Technology in Teaching   6   Using Internet resources

2.3.4 *Electronic mail: a convenient means of communication*

Email, as it is usually known, enables you to communicate conveniently and quickly with other computer users. Most sites have a dedicated mail server computer which sends, receives and stores email messages for its users. You log on to the mail server from a PC using your username and password for security. The email software shows you a list of messages received, which you can read, reply to, forward, store or delete. It is easy to send messages, providing you know the email addresses of the people you wish to contact. You can assign nicknames to individuals and groups to save having to remember their full addresses.

 Technology in Teaching   4.1   Electronic mail

2.3.5 *Remote login: using distant computers without leaving your desk*

Some facilities, such as high-performance supercomputer sites, are shared by researchers all over the world. Using software called Telnet you can use a computer on another continent as easily as you can use one in the next room. The commands you type are transmitted to a remote computer via the Internet, and its responses are sent back to be displayed on your screen. You can Telnet to any computer you are authorized to use.

 Technology in Teaching   3.5   Using Telnet to communicate with remote computers

2.3.6 *File transfer: retrieving useful files from distant computers*

Many computers on the Internet allow free access to some files, which you can copy to your computer. Facilities typically available include public-domain software and data archives. Software called ftp (file transfer protocol) allows you to log onto a remote computer, search the directories for the files you need and copy them to your local computer.

 Technology in Teaching   3.1   File transfer using ftp

Archie software enables a database of files available from ftp archives to be searched for items containing keywords, enabling specific files to be quickly found and accessed.

Technology in Teaching   3.2   Using Archie to search ftp archives

2.3.7 *Mailing lists: forums for discussion with like-minded people*

Email is used to run discussion lists and electronic journals on the Internet. There are over 4000 lists devoted to specific academic disciplines and other topics of more general interest. When you join a mailing list you will be sent a copy of every message posted to the list by its members. If you wish to respond to a message, you can email the list as a whole or just the person who posted the message. Popular discussion lists can easily generate more messages than you will have time to read.

Technology in Teaching   4.2   Mailing lists

2.3.8 *Usenet: an exchange of news and views open to all*

Usenet is another email-based technology used to facilitate discussion groups. There are currently over 20,000 'newsgroups' devoted to topics from the academic to the banal. Special newsreader software enables you to choose the newsgroups you wish to see and read new articles you are interested in. Messages often belong to various discussion 'threads', and the software makes it easy to follow these. Not all institutions provide access to Usenet.

Technology in Teaching   4.3   Usenet

2.3.9 *Gopher: browsing and retrieving information*

Gopher allows you to browse through structured menus of files held on remote computers by choosing menu items. You can transfer files back to your local PC by choosing the file you want from the menu. A Gopher menu can also list menus and files from other computers, effectively unifying their filestore. This has led to the creation of subject-based menus, which list related information on computers all over the world. This facility was enthusiastically adopted by the academic community to create a web of links, and the sum of these Gopher information sources has come to be known as GopherSpace.

Technology in Teaching   3.3   Using Gopher to access information on the Internet

Software called Veronica has been developed which allows a database of menu items to be searched for items containing keywords, thus enabling data stored on the Internet to be quickly and usefully searched and accessed.

Technology in Teaching 3.4 Veronica

2.3.10 *World Wide Web*

Much of the recent interest in the Internet has been caused by the rapid growth of information available on the World Wide Web, known as WWW or the Web. The Web is a distributed hypertext system – this means that links can be made between documents. Hypertext links appear as highlighted text when a document is viewed, and by clicking with the mouse on the link you activate it, which retrieves the linked document. You can thus easily follow up references and find related material, provided that it is available on the Web and has been properly linked.

Web documents are viewed using software called a Web browser, which runs on your local computer. The browser displays the Web documents and handles all communications with remote Web servers when you click on a link. Web documents are text files which use special codes called HTML to define their structure and links. The browser uses the HTML codes to display the document correctly, including graphics such as maps, graphs, diagrams and scanned photos. The Web browser can also work with other programs on the local computer to play sound and video files, and to display files created by other applications.

HTML codes allow forms to be created, so that you can type search queries, fill in questionnaires or even order pizza! Your responses can be automatically emailed to someone or added to a database. Technologies have been developed that enable secure transmission of data such as credit card numbers across the Internet, and these make a wide range of commercial transactions possible.

Setting up a Web server and creating HTML documents and related graphic files is relatively simple, so there has been an explosion in the number of sites on the Web. Increasingly and in large numbers, private individuals are connecting to the Internet via service providers, and the Web is the service they want to use. This growth looks likely to continue, although the Internet network is beginning to creak under the strain of the volume of data being moved, which leads to slow responses at peak times.

Technology in Teaching 5 Using the World Wide Web

2.4 How do you get connected?

The answer to this question depends on your PC, the network set-up at your institution, and the services you wish to use. For the purposes of this publication we assume that you

1 have a PC running DOS or Windows, or an Apple Macintosh
2 are not a computer 'expert' but can talk to your institution's IT service staff to find out about local facilities, services and requirements
3 want to use network services and resources to be found on JANET and the Internet.

The simplest way to get connected is, if possible, to get someone else to do it for you. For instance, your institution's IT service or your departmental network manager may be able to provide you with all the expertise and software you need to get up and running quickly. This is also likely to involve the use of standard equipment and procedures which will ultimately minimize any technical problems as well as simplifying their support role.

There are two main types of connection to networked services: gateway access and direct access. You may have a choice between them, or you may be constrained by your PC or your local network.

2.4.1 Gateway access

Gateway access means that your PC does not have a direct connection to the Internet but uses special software, called a terminal emulator, to control and communicate with a remote computer system (host) that is connected. The software installed on the remote host is used to communicate with and search the Internet, and to view information and retrieve files. The interface is text-only, so you either type commands at a prompt (like DOS or UNIX) or make choices from menus listing various options. Gateway access via a LAN or via a telephone line and modem requires two items of software:

– a terminal emulator to communicate with the host computer
– a file transfer package to copy files between your PC and the host computer.

| Technology in Teaching | 2.4.6 | What software do you need? |
| Technology in Teaching | 2.5 | About modem connections |

Some points you will need to bear in mind in relation to Internet access:

▲ There is now a general assumption by Internet service providers that users have modern PCs or workstations with direct access to the Internet. While it is still possible to use most services via a gateway and text-based interface, it is much less convenient than direct access.

▲ Inexperienced users often find typing commands confusing and difficult. However, you need to know only a few basic commands to be able to do useful work, and more experienced users can quickly carry out complex procedures using commands.

▲ Menu-based information systems are easy to use and offer a structured environment which can be helpful to inexperienced users. They provide a good starting point and encourage exploration of the options available.

▲ Gateway access performs acceptably over low-speed modem connections since relatively small amounts of data are transmitted.

▲ Gateway access does not require a modern PC to give acceptable performance: neither processor speed nor display quality are critical.

▲ Gateway access cannot retrieve files direct to your PC – you have to copy them to the remote host and then use file transfer software to copy them to your PC.

▲ Gateway access cannot display graphic files or exploit some of the other 'exciting' features offered on the World Wide Web.

▲ Only one task at a time can be performed with gateway access. This can be frustrating since some tasks (such as downloading a large file) can take quite a few minutes.

2.4.2 *Direct access*

With direct access your PC is connected directly to the Internet via a host computer. You use software installed on your PC, rather than the host, to communicate with and search the Internet, and to view information and retrieve files. Such software usually has a modern graphical interface and can therefore display graphics as well as text.

▲ Direct access via a LAN requires TCP/IP software to be installed on your PC to enable Internet communications.

▲ Direct access via a telephone line using a modem also requires software which supports either SLIP (Serial Line Internet Protocol) or PPP (Point-to-Point Protocol). The choice may be dictated by the service provider, but, if you have the choice, we recommend PPP as a newer, faster technology.

▲ The installation and configuration of all this software can be fairly complex, especially on DOS and Windows PCs.

▲ Note that you will also need additional software to allow you to use email, the World Wide Web and other Internet services.

Technology in Teaching   2.4.6   What software do you need?

Technology in Teachign   2.5   About modem connections

Issues to consider:

▲ Modern software provides a sophisticated, easy-to-use interface to the services available. This not only benefits inexperienced users but also offers control over advanced features which can significantly enhance the services on offer.

▲ To give satisfactory performance you will need a modern PC (a Windows PC or an Apple Macintosh) to run the software.

▲ Direct access using a modem connection requires a fast modem – 28.8 kbps (kilobits per second) at least – especially if you want to view Web pages containing graphic images.

▲ Direct access enables you to retrieve files directly to your PC.

▲ You can carry out several tasks at once – for example, you can use email or browse the World Wide Web while at the same time retrieving a large file.

2.4.3 *Three typical scenarios*

In this section we consider three scenarios and suggest solutions for each:

▲ **Networked PC**
Your PC is connected to either a departmental or campus network.

▲ **Non-networked PC**
Your office PC is not connected to a network (or you simply do not have a PC).

▲ **Home PC**
You have a PC at home.

Networked PC
As you already have a network connection, your IT service department may have installed software on your PC which give easy access to local information and services such as email. You may also be able to use central computer systems which allow gateway access to the Internet – this is probably your best option, if your PC is unable to run modern software.

You will need to talk to your institution's IT service or departmental LAN manager to find out what services, advice and software are available. They may be able to provide the necessary software, and help with installation and configuration – they may also be able to offer some training to get you started.

Most networks are based on Ethernet technology which also allows TCP/IP communications, so it should be possible to gain direct access to the Internet and all the advantages that brings. The basic software requirements are as follows:

▲ a unique Internet address for your PC: this will be assigned by your institution's IT service

▲ TCP/IP software, to enable your PC to communicate with the Internet

▲ mail client software, to read, send and organize email

▲ web-browser software so that you can use the World Wide Web.

You could also install additional software, such as:

▲ news reader software, to manage any newsgroup to which you subscribe

▲ file decompression software, which automatically unpacks files retrieved from the Internet (files are usually compressed to minimise the storage space required and the amount of data transferred)

▲ 'helper' applications, which work with the Web browser to enable you to view various other file types, such as PostScript files, Adobe Acrobat files, Director animation files and so on. (Some of these features may be integrated with future releases of some Web browsers.)

Non-networked PC

If you do not have a PC, you should be able to use public-access PCs (workstations provided mainly for use by students) provided by your institution's IT service. These PCs will almost certainly be connected to a LAN, and probably to a campus network and the Internet. Contact the service's help desk or advisory service to find out what facilities they provide, and ask about email, file transfer and World Wide Web browsers. One disadvantage of this arrangement is that you may not always find a free workstation when you want to use one, and another is that you cannot 'personalize' the software (for example, by creating fast-access 'bookmark' lists of interesting Web sites you have found and wish to re-visit).

If you do have a PC in your office, but is not networked, you have two choices:

▲ Arrange to put your PC on the network. This is the best option, but may not be possible if your PC or office location is unsuitable, or if your departmental budget cannot afford it.

▲ Buy a modem and arrange dial-up access to a remote computer. You may be able to use the internal telephone system to connect to a host computer at your site, so access will be 'free'. Alternatively you may have to use a commercial service, in which case you will have to pay for the initial telephone connection, then a monthly service charge and probably a usage charge.

Technology in Teaching   2.4.4   Commercial Internet service providers (ISPs)

The type of access you get with the latter option depends on the host computer: if the host can handle SLIP or PPP connections then you will have direct access to the Internet – otherwise you will have to use gateway access.

Two items of software are required for gateway access via a modem – a terminal emulator to communicate with the host computer and a file transfer package to copy files between your PC and the host computer.

The basic software requirements for direct access via a modem are as follows:

▲ TCP/IP software, to enable your PC to communicate with the Internet

▲ SLIP or PPP software to handle TCP/IP communications using a modem

▲ mail client software, to read, send and organize email

▲ web-browser software so that you can use the World Wide Web.

Technology in Teaching   2.4.1   Gateway access

Again, your first step is to talk to your institution's IT service or departmental LAN manager, who should be able to advise you on the services, advice and software available, and may be able to provide help with installation and configuration, and perhaps even training.

Home PC
Really the only way to connect your home PC to the Internet is via a modem and telephone line. The cheapest option is to connect to your institution's host computers (provided that dial-up access to them is possible) in which case the only cost will be the telephone call. Your institution's IT service will be able to tell you what services, advice and software are available. The basic software requirements are the same as those for the non-networked PC situation described above.

2.4.4   *Commercial Internet service providers (ISPs)*

If dial-up access to your institution is not possible you will have to use a commercial service provider. You will have to pay for the telephone connection, a monthly service charge and additional usage charges, since it is unlikely that your department will pay for these. Commercial services normally provide all the software required and instructions on how to install it. (The software is often shareware and you may have to pay a registration fee to the author in order to use the software legally, but some services include this for you.)

When deciding which Internet service provider to choose, ask the following questions:

▲ How much does the service cost?
Some companies charge a flat monthly rate irrespective of how long you spend on-line, while others make a monthly charge which includes a fixed amount of free time on-line and then charge for any extra time by the minute. Most commercial services require payment by credit card, but some (such as CompuServe) also allow accounts to be set up by companies.

▲ Where is the nearest point of presence (PoP)?
This is the location of the telephone number(s) which you dial to connect to the service provider. A PoP which is only a local call away will help to keep your telephone bill down.

▲ Does the service provider's PoP support your modem speed?
Fast modems cost little more than older, slower models and can quickly pay for themselves by reducing the amount of time you need to spend on-line.

▲ Will the ISP provide adequate software and telephone support?
Some offer complete user-friendly interfaces to their services, while others provide as little as a couple of disks of unregistered shareware.

▲ Does the service provider support the connection protocols you need?
SLIP and PPP provide direct access, while POP3 allows off-line email handling.

In July 1997 there were around 200 UK commercial services offering Internet access. For up-to-date details (including costs and contact numbers), see the current issue of a UK Internet magazine such as *.net* or *Internet*, which feature directories of ISPs. To give you an idea of the range of services available from large and small organizations, here are details of three ISPs:

CompuServe offers information and services in addition to direct Internet access. Its software for the Windows PC or Apple Macintosh provides an attractive, easy-to-use interface to their services and is an ideal introduction to networked services for computer novices. An off-line reader is provided for email. Full Internet connectivity is available, although CompuServe censors some sites and services – those responsible for children who have Internet access would probably consider this a good option.

The basic charge is around £6.50 (CompuServe charge in dollars, so the sterling amount varies with the exchange rate) per month, which includes five hours' use of 'basic' services and about 90 email messages (incoming or outgoing), plus around £1.95 for each extra hour on-line. Alternatively, you can pay about £16.30 per month, which allows for 20 hours' use, and a further £1.25 for each extra hour. Some 'premium' (commercial) services carry an extra charge, ranging from £5 to £10 per use.

CompuServe has eight PoPs in major cities, with cheap connections via Mercury or GNS DialPlus from locations throughout the UK. Its modems now support 36.6 kbps. For full details email *70006.101@compuserve.com* or telephone 0800 289378.

Demon is the largest UK Internet service and is also the cheapest to use. Direct Internet access is provided, together with a useful archive of software. The service is very busy and access can be a problem, particularly in the evenings. However, the company's popularity means that it has the necessary income to upgrade its services to cope with demand.

The start-up fee is £12.50 and there is a flat monthly charge of £10 (plus VAT). Demon has 114 PoPs, which give local-call access for 98% of the UK population. It can support all modem speeds up to 28.8 kbps. Either email Demon at *sales@demon.net* or telephone 0181 371 1234.

Aladdin is a small ISP, based in the Southampton area, with just one PoP. Aladdin is a typical small ISP, in that it offers a range of services tailored to individuals and businesses, as well as ISDN and cable-phone links. It also provides reduced connection charges to CompuServe, space on its Web server and local support. The start-up fee is £23.50 and there is a flat monthly charge of £10. Modems up to 28.8 kbps are supported. Either email *info@aladdin.co.uk* or telephone 01489 782221.

2.4.5   *How to obtain the necessary software*

All the software you need can be downloaded from the Internet! However, to start off with, you can try the following sources:

▲ A friend, colleague, LAN manager or IT service who already has the software. This is probably the easiest option and ensures a degree of standardization with others in your department or institution.

▲ A magazine cover disk. Many PC and Internet magazines give away software in this way, but you may find you have to consult a number of magazines to find one with the software you want. You may also need access to a PC with a CD-ROM drive, as cover disks are often provided as CD-ROMs.

▲ A book. Some Internet books come complete with the software described in their text. This option may well be the most useful for novices, as the books give advice on installing and using the software. Of the many books now available, two which include the necessary software and have received good reviews are:

– *The Internet Starter Kit for Windows* by Adam Engst, Corwin Low and Michael Simon, published by Hayden, ISBN 1-56830-094-8, price £30. This comes with Winsock (TCP/IP software), Chameleon (WWW browser), WinVN (newsreader), Eudora (email reader), WS Gopher (Gopher browser), and other useful items

– *The Internet Starter Kit for Macintosh* (2nd edition) by Adam Engst, published by Hayden, ISBN 1-56830-111-1, price £30. This comes with MacTCP (TCP/IP software), MacPPP, InterSLIP, Eudora, MacWeb (WWW browser), TurboGopher (Gopher browser), and other useful items.

▲ On-line software archives. Two good UK archives are:

Higher Education National Software Archive (HENSA)
ftp address: *micros.hensa.ac.uk*
Web address: *http://www.hensa.ac.uk*

SunSITE at the Department of Computing, Imperial College, London
ftp address: *src.doc.ic.ac.uk*
Web address: *http://src.doc.ic.ac.uk*

2.4.6 *What software do you need?*

The software suggested in this section is probably the best choice at the moment. The publication of new software and updated versions, plus other factors (such as personal preference) mean that you should not regard this list as definitive. Where practicable we have suggested low-cost shareware – in many cases it is as good as commercial products, and some is free to academic users!

It is a good idea to talk to your institution's IT service or departmental network manager before purchasing any software. They probably support selected packages only – so if you buy an alternative they will not be able to help you if you run into problems. On a more positive note, they may be able to recommend and supply software at an educational discount. The Combined Higher Education Software Team (CHEST) has negotiated deals with the suppliers of many popular software packages, so always ask whether special prices are available.

Software for DOS PCs
PCs that can only use DOS (ie not Windows) can be tricky to configure for Internet access.

▲ If you just need gateway access via a modem you will have to obtain a DOS terminal emulator, since all modern modems come with Windows software. You will also have to configure the software to work with your modem – but it may not support the full capabilities of the modem. This configuration will mean hand editing initialization files while trying to understand uninformative help files. You have been warned! The recommended software is called Kermit and is free – ask your local IT service for a copy.

▲ If you need direct access, you also need to be (or to know) an expert. Windows allows the use of generic TCP/IP software like Winsock, but with DOS you need a 'packet driver' to work with the Ethernet card. You need the right version of the right software to work with your particular make and model of Ethernet card!

Getting this to work correctly is something of a black art. After that it will come as no surprise that we recommend that you buy a new Windows PC or an Apple Macintosh if you have a DOS PC and wish to use the Internet.

Software for Windows PCs

If you only require gateway access to the Internet via a modem link, you can use the terminal emulation software provided with your modem. This may also have Xmodem or Zmodem capabilities that make it possible to download files from the remote host. You could also use the Terminal program supplied with Windows 3.1. If you only require gateway access via a network, you will need Telnet (eg WinQVT/net) and TCP/IP (eg Trumpet Winsock) software.

Windows software can provide a sophisticated, easy-to-use interface to Internet facilities such as email and the World Wide Web. You will need additional system software that enables Windows to use TCP/IP communications – but luckily a standard called Winsock has emerged. Many Internet client programs use this Winsock standard, greatly simplifying their installation and configuration. Note that Windows 95 comes with its own Winsock.

A complete and detailed list of all the Windows client programs that offer access to Internet facilities using the Winsock interface is contained in a regularly-updated document called 'The Windows Client Listing' by Ed Sinkovits. The latest update of this list is available from the following prime location under the file name winterXX.zip (where XX is the version):
ftp://oak.oakland.edu/SimTel/win3/winsock/winterXX.zip

It is also available from HENSA – look in the Windows software archive under the keyword WINSOCK for the WINSOCK CLIENT LISTING.

Some client applications (NCSA Mosaic and Netscape in particular) also require additional system software called Win32s that allows Windows 3 to act as a 32-bit operating system. Microsoft have made this software freely available and it can be downloaded from most software archives. Windows 95 is a genuine 32-bit system and does not require Win32s.

Software type	Product	Cost for academic use
TCP/IP + SLIP + PPP	Trumpet Winsock 2.0	$25
Telnet and more	WinQVT/net	$45
Telnet and more	LAN Workplace for Windows	£10 (plus about £80 for the manuals)
FTP	WS_FTP	Free
Email	Eudora Lite	Free
Newsreader	Free Agent	Free
Gopher	WS_Gopher	Free
World Wide Web browser	Microsoft Internet Explorer	Free
World Wide Web browser	Netscape Navigator	Free

TCP/IP + SLIP + PPP Make sure that you get version 2.0 of this software if you need PPP support.

Telnet Both WinQVT/net and LAN Workplace for Windows offer more than simple telnet facilities. WinQVT/net also includes software for email (POP3 and SMTP), newsreader, ftp, remote printing and three server applications that allow other Internet users to access your PC. LAN Workplace also includes software for ftp (including an ftp server) as well as various useful Internet utilities.

FTP, Newsreader and Gopher WS_FTP can work with another free program, WS_Archie, that provides Archie search facilities. Note that web browsers such as Netscape and Mosaic can also act as ftp, Newsreader and Gopher clients, so you do not really need this software as well.

Email Eudora Lite is a reasonably powerful, easy-to-use shareware mail client that uses the POP3 protocol. There is a commercial version, Eudora Pro, which comes with extra features, manuals and telephone support.

Web browser The most popular package is Netscape, which fully supports not only the HTML standard but also many non-standard (but widely used) enhancements. There are also lots of commercial browsers, based on NCSA Mosaic, which are provided with books or by commercial service providers.

Software for the Apple Macintosh
If you only require gateway access to the Internet via a modem link, you can use the terminal emulation software provided with your modem. This may also have Xmodem or Zmodem capabilities that make it possible to download files from the remote host. ZTerm ($30) is the best shareware terminal emulator and is supplied with many modems.

If you only require gateway access via a network, you will need telnet (NCSA Telnet) and TCP/IP (MacTCP) software.

Macintosh software can provide a sophisticated, easy-to-use interface to Internet facilities such as email and the World Wide Web. You will need additional system software called MacTCP that enables your Macintosh to use TCP/IP communications. This is now provided as standard with System 7.5 and is often included with other client software that requires it. One of the cheapest and easiest ways to obtain a legal copy is to buy the Internet book mentioned in Technology 2.4.5.

Software type	Product	Cost for academic use
TCP/IP	MacTCP	$25
SLIP	InterSLIP	Free
PPP	MacPPP	Free
Telnet	NCSA Telnet	Free
FTP	Anarchie	$10
Email	Eudora Lite	Free
Newsreader	NewsHopper	£39
Gopher	TurboGopher	Free
World Wide Web browser	NCSA Mosaic	Free
World Wide Web browser	Netscape Navigator	Free

FTP, Newsreader and Gopher Anarchie integrates an Archie search tool with ftp. If you just need ftp, a free program called Fetch is recommended. Note that web browsers such as Netscape and Mosaic can also act as ftp, Newsreader and Gopher clients, so you do not really need separate software for this as well.

Email Eudora is a reasonably powerful, easy-to-use shareware mail client that uses the POP3 protocol. There is a commercial version, Eudora Pro, which comes with extra features, manuals and support.

Web browser The most popular package is Netscape, which fully supports not only the HTML standard but also many non-standard (but widely used) enhancements.

2.5   *About modem connections*

A modem is a piece of computer hardware that converts the digital information used by your computer into sounds that can be sent down an ordinary phone line. Another modem between the remote computer and the phone line turns the sounds back into digital information. Advances in technology have vastly increased both the speed and reliability of data transmission. Don't buy a modem that has a communication speed of less than 14.4 kbps (kilobits per second) and 28.8 kbps is recommended for browsing the World Wide Web.

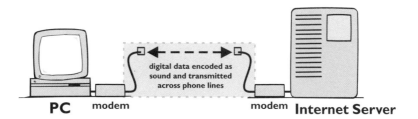

Most modern modems are described as 'fax-modems' and are sold with software that allows you to send a fax from your PC almost as easily as printing a document. Many models are also capable of receiving faxes, although this usually means you have to leave your computer on all the time! You may also need to have a separate phone line dedicated to data communications.

There are two basic types of dial-up connection:

▲ **Gateway access** This option is simple to set up and use. Most modems are sold with the terminal emulation and file transfer software required.

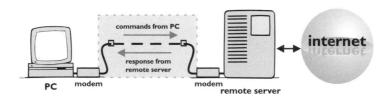

▲ **Direct access** This option is more difficult to set up and requires additional software to be acquired, installed and configured.

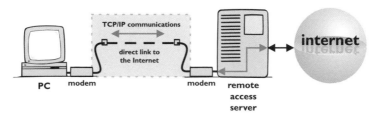

With direct access you will need SLIP (Serial Line Interface Protocol) or PPP (Point-to-Point) software that enables your computer to use TCP/IP communications over a phone line. PPP is recommended if you have the choice.

Technology in Teaching	2.4.1	Gateway access (for more about these types of connection)
Technology in Teaching	2.4.2	Direct access

3   Using Internet resources

In this chapter you will find information on using the Internet to locate and retrieve resources stored in databases, text and software archives on remote computers. These major techniques and software applications are discussed:

▲ File transfer, used to copy files to and from remote computers

▲ Archie, a database of publicly accessible files, which you can interrogate to find the exact location of the files you require

▲ Gopher, an easy-to-use menu-based interface to Internet resources

▲ Veronica, a database of Gopher resources, which you can query to find the exact location of the information you need

▲ Telnet, used to access and control remote computers which you have permission to use

▲ WAIS, used to find information by searching a database holding the content of a collection of documents.

Some general advice is also given on making your own information available on the Internet.

A major exclusion is information on the World Wide Web, which is covered in detail in chapter 5 Using the World Wide Web.

3.1   *File transfer using ftp*

You pronounce ftp as it is spelt: eff tee pee

File transfer means copying files (not only over the Internet) from one computer to another. The name of the Internet protocol used to handle these transfers is ftp (file transfer protocol) and this acronym is also used as a verb (meaning to transfer over the Internet). You may come across people saying, for example: 'You can ftp the file from this software archive' or 'Could you ftp the file to me, please'.

Using ftp to transfer files involves logging on to a remote computer, searching for the file you need and then copying it to your computer (PC or UNIX account); this is known as downloading the file. Alternatively, you may be allowed to copy a file from your computer to the remote computer; this is known as uploading the file.

You normally need a valid username and password to login to a remote computer. However, there are many data and software archives (often simply called ftp sites) which are available to anyone, provided you login with the special username *anonymous*. This is what is meant when you hear that 'software xyz is available by anonymous ftp from this archive'. A password is not mandatory, but it is polite to enter your full email address as the password so that the archive's managers can see who is using their service.

When you login to an ftp site as *anonymous* you are automatically restricted to using a safe sub-set of UNIX commands within directories specified as publicly available by the site's managers. These restrictions are necessary for obvious security reasons. If you only have gateway access to the Internet you can use the UNIX ftp program to transfer files. Consult your institution's IT service for information on using this program.

3.1.1 Using modern ftp programs

These days there are many programs that hide the rather cryptic UNIX ftp commands behind a modern user interface. You can either get a specialized ftp program or use the ftp capabilities built into most Web browsers, such as Mosaic and Netscape.

For PCs, the most popular ftp programs are probably WS_FTP and CuteFTP for Windows and Fetch and Anarchie for Macintosh, all of which are low-cost shareware obtainable from ftp software archives. You can avoid the chicken-and-egg problem this poses by getting these programs from the disks included with computing magazines or Internet books. Alternatively, ask your institution's IT service for a copy. Once you have connected to the remote computer, these programs enable you to browse through its directories and copy files using the same techniques that you already use with your PC's file management system. In effect, the ftp site's file structure becomes an extension of your local computer network.

The software has many convenient features such as configuration files that store all the connection details for ftp sites, making reconnection as easy as choosing their name from a menu. On-line help is provided as a convenient alternative to a printed manual.

WS_FTP has a dialogue box that allows you to save the addresses and connection details for the ftp sites you use regularly. It can also automate anonymous login.

FTP Client Connect to...	☒
Config name: hensa ▼	**Retry:** 0
Host name: micros.hensa.ac.uk	**Timeout:** 65
Host type: auto detect ▼	**Port:** 21
User ID: anonymous	☑ Anonymous Login
Password: *********************	☑ Save Password
Account:	☐ Use Firewall
Remote Dir:	☐ Auto save config
Local Dir:	
Init Cmd:	Set Firewall Info
Save Config	Delete Config	Help	Cancel	OK

Once you are connected to the ftp site, WS_FTP makes it easy to move around remote and local directories and select files to copy.

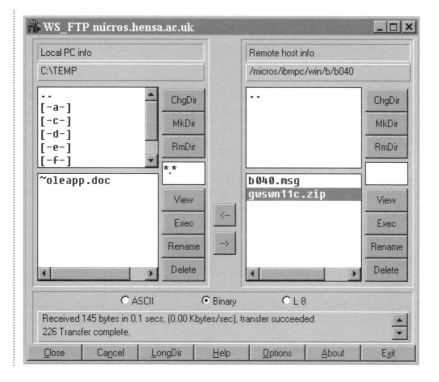

3.2   Using Archie to search ftp archives

Most ftp sites organise their files using a tree structure to help people find what they are looking for. However, searching an ftp site manually can be very time consuming and frustrating unless you know precisely which file you are looking for and the location of the directory in which it is stored. Take into account the fact that there are thousands of ftp sites and you realize the scale of the search involved.

You will be relieved to learn that there is a quick and simple way to find the exact location(s) of any file you need. Archie is a database of all the files held by all the anonymous ftp sites on the Internet. This database is searchable, so all you need to do is tell it what you are looking for and it will tell you where to find it.

There are a number of computers (servers) around the world that hold the complete Archie database. Each Archie server regularly gathers details of all the files held by all the anonymous ftp sites in one (or more) Internet domains. For example, the UK Archie server keeps track of Australian ftp sites and the Australian Archie server keeps track of UK ftp sites. Every month, Archie servers all around the world exchange data so that they all have a complete up-to-date database.

To minimise network traffic, always try to use the nearest Archie server. For a list of these, see http://sunsite.doc.ic.ac.UK/archie/archie.html The UK Archie server is run by Imperial College in London and its address is: archie.doc.ic.ac.uk

If you only have gateway access to the Internet you can use Telnet to log on to an Archie server and then type commands that set options and specify the search. Consult your institution's IT service for information on using Telnet and Archie.

3.2.1 Using modern Archie programs

Archie software is available that hides the Telnet connection and Archie commands behind a modern user interface. For PCs, the most popular programs are WS_Archie for Windows (from the same people who developed the WS_ftp described in Technology 3.1.1) and Anarchie for Macintosh, both of which are low-cost shareware obtainable from ftp software archives. You can either get these programs from the disks included with many computing magazines and Internet books, or you can ask your institution's IT service for a copy.

WS_Archie integrates well with WS_ftp to help you download the files you want. Anarchie includes an ftp client to provide a complete search-and-get solution.

WS_Archie makes it easy to specify the type and scope of a search, and presents the results in an easy-to-use format.

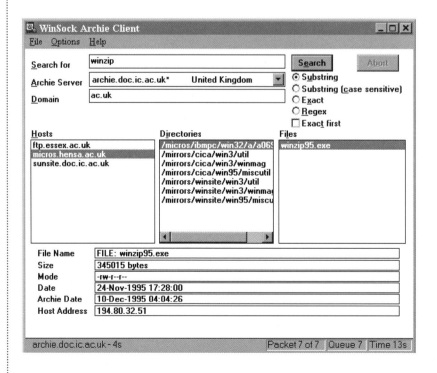

The screenshot above shows how the software:
- enables you to specify the Archie server by selecting it from a drop-down list
- makes it easy to specify the type and target of the search – the on-line help explains the differences between the various types and how best to use them
- makes it easy to limit the network domain to be searched without typing in Archie options
- displays the results in a much more convenient fashion than the long list generated by the Archie server.

3.3   *Using Gopher to access information on the Internet*

Gopher (pronounced go-fur) was developed at the University of Minnesota as a way of providing its staff and students with easy-to-use text-menu access to its ftp site's resources. Use quickly spread until Gopher became the Internet's first interactive navigation and indexing system. It is still in widespread use today, although it is being replaced by the World Wide Web.

Gopher uses client–server techniques to access and display files from remote computers. A piece of software called a Gopher client running on your PC communicates across the Internet with Gopher servers running on remote computers. This sequence of events describes how the client and servers interact:

1 When your client connects to a server, it sends a message requesting a file containing a menu of options.
2 The server sends this file across the Internet and your client displays the menu.
3 When you select one of the options from the menu, your client sends another message to the server requesting the file corresponding to that option. This file can contain either another menu or actual data (text, images, etc).
4 The server sends this file and your client displays it.

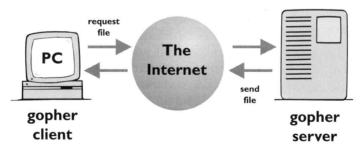

In practice, using Gopher is simply a matter of selecting menu options until you find the information you are looking for, as illustrated by these screenshots of a search for back-issues of EDUPAGE, an electronic journal:

The WS_Gopher client has connected to the BUBL (BUlletin Board for Libraries) Gopher server and is displaying BUBL's top-level menu. The icons to the left of each option show whether they are menus or a data file.

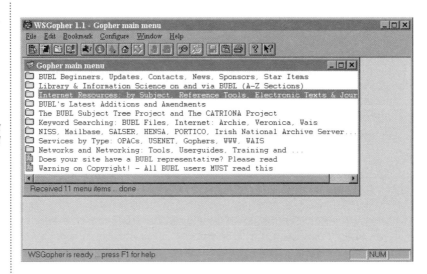

Double-clicking on an option automatically downloads its associated menu or file, which appears in a new sub-window. You can access any menu by clicking on its sub-window title bar.

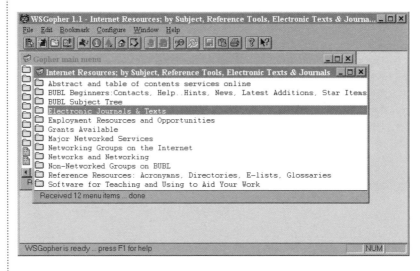

WS_Gopher can automatically 'cascade' the menu sub-windows so that you can easily see how you reached your current menu – or return to a previous menu.

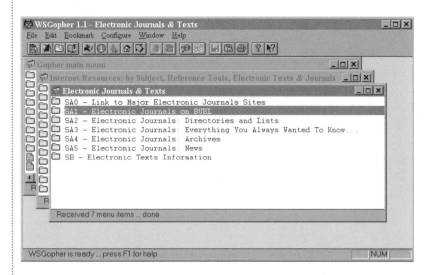

It seems that BUBL has an archive containing EDUPAGE, the electronic journal that we are looking for.

This menu is a list of all the back issues, each of which is a single text file.

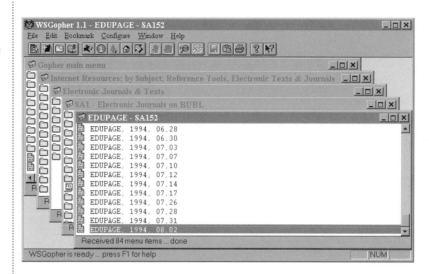

Double-clicking on the option for the latest issue downloads the file and displays it in its own sub-window. You may either print this file or save it to your PC's hard disk.

What this quick search did not show was that menu options do not have to be files on the same remote computer, but can refer to any file on any Internet Gopher server. A menu option on one server can lead to a menu on another server, which means that all the resources of all the Gopher servers in the world are (potentially) seamlessly linked. This world of linked information is known as GopherSpace.

The availability of a menu bringing together resources stored on other Gopher servers quickly led to the development of subject-based menus. For example, a geophysical sciences menu may have options which link to useful geophysics resources anywhere in GopherSpace. At another site, someone creating a geography resources menu might include a link to that geophysical sciences menu – and so on. Much of the value of GopherSpace is due to this collating and indexing of information sources.

The most popular Gopher client programs are WS_Gopher for Windows PCs and TurboGopher for Macintosh PCs. These are low-cost shareware obtainable from ftp software archives, from the disks accompanying many computing magazines and Internet books, or from your institution's IT service. Web browsers such as Netscape and Mosaic can also be used to navigate GopherSpace and view files.

Gopher client programs have modern features such as a toolbar for the most used functions, on-line help and a bookmark list for fast access to a wide range of Gopher servers. Interesting menus or files can be easily added to the bookmark list for future reference.

3.4   Veronica

Browsing through Gopher menus is a slow, hit and miss way of searching for specific information. Subject-based menus can provide a good starting point for browsing, but you can never be sure what you have missed. A better solution is to search a database containing all the menu entries and document titles in GopherSpace. This database is called Veronica and is assembled and updated in much the same way as the Archie database of ftp sites described in Technology 3.2.

For further information on Veronica, go to gopher://gopher.micro.umn.edu/and follow the link to 'Other Gopher and information servers'. Then choose 'Search titles in Gopherspace using Veronica'.

You will often find a link to Veronica from the top-level menu of Gopher sites. Look for options such as:

▲ Search GopherSpace using Veronica

▲ Other Gopher and information services.

This screenshot shows the BUBL menus that led to this keyword search window:

You may be presented with a list of sites that offer Veronica searches, as well as files giving information about the Veronica database and how to use it.

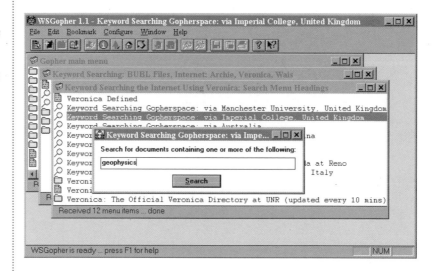

This search on *geophysics* found 201 entries, which demonstrates how important it is to define clearly what you want as exactly as possible. If you enter multiple terms, Veronica will only find those menus and files whose titles contain all the keywords. For example, searching for *geophysics astronomy* found only 18 entries.

You can tailor the search in a number of ways to ensure that you find only the items you actually want. There is usually a help file which explains the options and their use in some detail, but here are the essentials:

▲ search keywords are not case-sensitive

▲ you can search for particular types of resource, such as text files or GIF image files

▲ you can create more complex searches such as *politics (feminist or women) not green* which would find items whose titles contained the words politics and feminist or politics and women, but not the word green

▲ you can use the wildcard characters to search using parts of words. For example *astro** would find items whose titles included the words astronomy, astrology, astronautics, etc.

The results of the search are displayed as a standard Gopher menu, so it is easy to look at the resources found and see whether they are what you need.

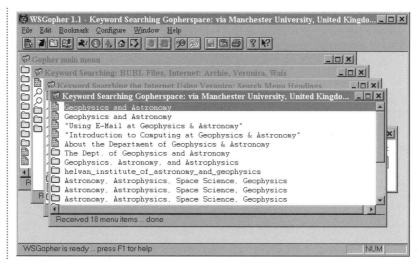

3.5 Using Telnet to communicate with remote computers

Telnet is also used as a verb: for example, "You can telnet to this site."

Telnet enables you to communicate with and control remote computers (often called hosts) across the Internet. For example, if you had permission to use a computer in Hong Kong, you could use Telnet to log in to that computer from your office PC in the UK. You would be able to use all the facilities and software normally available on that computer, including saving files to its filestore.

Using Telnet to control a remote computer is often called remote access.

Using Telnet, it makes no difference whether the remote host is in the next room or the other side of the world – except for the speed of response. It may take a few seconds for the commands you type to find their way across the Internet to the remote host, and a few more seconds for the computer's response to be relayed back and displayed on your PC screen.

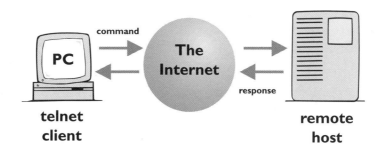

As a text-based interface, Telnet is ideal for communicating with UNIX hosts. If the remote host also provides a modern graphical X-windows interface such as OSF/Motif or SUN's OpenLook, it is possible to use a program such as Vista eXceed to display and use this interface on your client PC. Ask your institution's IT service for further details if you need this type of access.

There are several situations in which you might use Telnet to access remote computers:

▲ When visiting another institution you can telnet to your home site, log on to your UNIX account and use email or other software.

▲ You may be able to obtain an account on a remote host in connection with your work. For example, you might need to use the processing power provided by national or international supercomputer sites. If you do need this, your department or computing service should be able to help you arrange it.

▲ Some institutions allow public Internet access to their databases, possibly using a Gopher server to make finding and retrieving information easier (see Technology 3.3). When you telnet to these sites you will often be told what username to use to access their services (eg *guest* or *gopher* or *library*). This is done so as to control what public users can see and do – in a similar way to the *anonymous* ftp username.

3.5.1 Using the UNIX Telnet program

If you have an account on a UNIX computer, you can use the telnet host_address command to start the program and connect to the host. For example:

```
user>telnet solaris.soton.ac.uk
```
The host responds by inviting you to log in by entering your username:
```
UNIX(r) System V Release 4.0 (oak)
login: xyz
```
It then asks you to enter your password, which is not displayed as you type it:
```
Password:
```

If your username and password are valid, the login is completed and you have access to the system:
```
Last login: Wed Dec 13 14:59:07
xyz:~>
```

When you have finished, log out in the normal way to close the connection to the remote host:
```
xyz:~>exit
```

If the host stops responding to your commands, you can get back to the telnet> prompt by typing the Escape command. This is often Ctrl] – ie hold down the

Ctrl key and tap the] (close square brackets) key. At the `telnet` prompt you can type `close` to break the connection and log out:

```
telnet>close
```

You can open a new connection to the same (or another) host by typing the `open host_address` command – for example:

```
telnet>open archie.doc.ic.ac.uk
```

The quit command will enable you to exit from the telnet program:

```
telnet>quit
```

3.5.2   *Using Telnet on PCs*

There are many programs that allow PCs on the Internet to use Telnet for remote access. Some of these programs come as part of commercial Internet suites such as LAN Workplace (for DOS and Windows), while others are stand-alone shareware or freeware programs such as WinQVTnet for Windows and NCSA Telnet for Macintosh.

WinQVTnet offers Telnet, ftp, a Usenet news reader and an email program, all accessed from a toolbar:

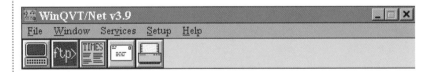

Clicking on the first button launches the Telnet program and displays a dialog box that allows you to enter a host's address or choose one from a list of sites that you have already visited:

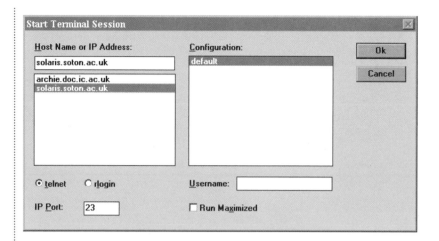

Clicking on the OK button connects to the site and opens a Telnet terminal window so that you can log in by typing your username and password:

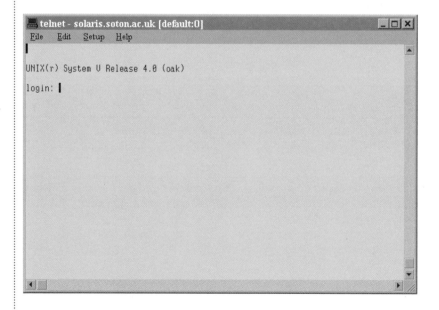

This window closes automatically when you close the connection to the remote host. The software has useful features such as the facility to configure the appearance of the window (fonts, sizes, colours) and to save a complete record of the session to a log file for later use.

3.6 WAIS

WAIS is pronounced ways.

WAIS (Wide Area Information Server) is different from Archie (see Technology 3.2) and Veronica (see Technology 3.4) in that it enables you to search a collection of documents at a site and find those which are most likely to contain the information you are looking for. It can do this because the WAIS database effectively contains an index of all the text in all the documents. When you put a query to the database, WAIS first finds all the documents that contain your search terms. It then looks at how often the search terms appear in each document and uses this to create a list ranking the documents in the probable order of relevance. WAIS systems are almost always accessed via Gopher or the World Wide Web, so the list has links which give one-click access to the actual documents.

A 'search engine' is jargon for software used to search a database.

WAIS is the most common 'search engine' used for searching text files on the Internet, so whenever you see a Gopher menu option or Web link that says something like *Search this University's Resources*, or *Search Electronic Journal text archive*, you're probably using WAIS software.

WAIS is really just another Internet communication protocol that specifies how WAIS client software should interact with WAIS servers. Several WAIS servers are available, each with different capabilities. The original WAIS, often called the 'b5' version, was released by Thinking Machines, Inc. In addition there is IUBio WAIS from Indiana University, and the freeware freeWAIS from CNIDR (Clearinghouse for Networked Information Discovery and Retrieval). Another freeware program called Harvest is also used as a WAIS server, although it has other capabilities.

This example shows how a collection of documents held by NISS (National Information on Software and Services) relating to the Follett Report on UK academic libraries was searched for items relating to the search terms 'multimedia' and 'internet':

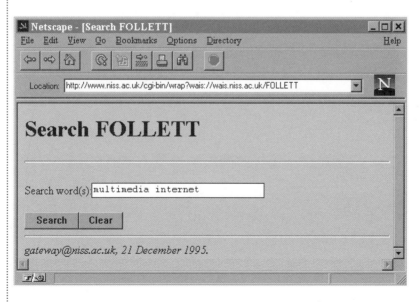

The WAIS server returns a list of documents containing the search terms.

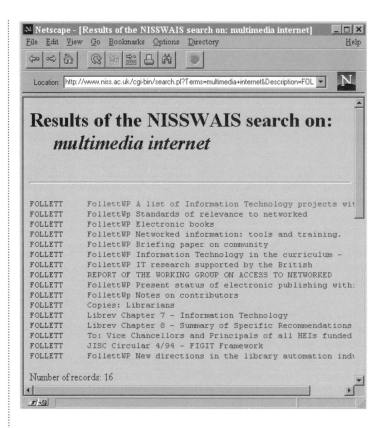

Clicking on the first document retrieves and displays it so that you can see if it is relevant. You can check the other documents just as easily.

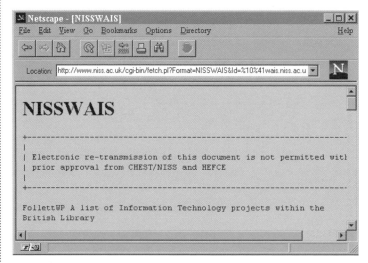

The original WAIS 'b5' software effectively performs an OR search (ie in the example it would find all documents containing the words *multimedia* OR *internet*). The IUBio software allows more complex searches using the Boolean operators AND, NOT, OR – provided they are capitalised (ie you could search for all documents containing the words *multimedia* AND *internet*, but NOT the word *fish*). The freeWAIS software allows uncapitalised Boolean operators and word-stems (ie you could use the search term *photo** to find documents containing the words *photo, photon, photograph, photographer*, etc).

Unfortunately, you cannot tell what type of software is being used for a WAIS search, so formulating queries can be a problem.

▲ Always look for any on-line help supplied, which should tell you what types of search are possible.

▲ Failing that, it is safest to assume that you are using the original WAIS and cannot use Boolean searches. This means that you should only search for single terms – unless you really want to look for documents containing *this* OR *that* OR *the other*.

▲ You can mimic a word-stem search by specifying all the words in which you are interested – for example, *photo photograph photographs*.

▲ A search for a very specific term often produces fewer but more relevant results than a search for lots of related terms. For example, if you were looking for information on the VT100 terminal emulator protocol you should search for *VT100* rather than *VT100 terminal emulator protocol* – which would also find documents about other protocols or ones that simply used the word terminal (probably in its other meanings).

3.7   *Making your own material available on the Internet*

You may have software, text documents, image files or data resources that you would like to make available on the Internet. While it is outside the scope of this publication to describe in detail how to do this, here is some general advice.

It is your responsibility to ensure either that you own the copyright of the materials or that you have explicit written permission to make them available in this way.

Using Technology   1.3   Copyright and intellectual property rights

If your data contains information about individuals you must make sure that you comply with the Data Protection Act.

Basic considerations

▲ The materials must always be available, so the computer that they are stored on must be switched on and connected to the Internet 24 hours a day.

▲ The computer must be running server software (eg ftp server, Gopher server, Web server). This is available for PCs, but may mean that the computer cannot be used for normal purposes.

▲ If you run your own server you need to be aware of many security considerations. Any computer server connected to the Internet is vulnerable to hackers and care needs to be taken to ensure that it is as secure as possible.

▲ The easiest way for you to make your material available is therefore to do so by using the resources provided by your institution's IT service. It probably already has UNIX systems running the server software and permanently connected to the Internet; it will also have the expertise needed to keep these systems secure.

Anonymous ftp

If the material is currently stored on a PC you will need to copy it to a filestore which is accessible by the ftp server, such as the filestore belonging to your UNIX account, if you have one. If your PC has Internet access, you can do this using ftp. Once the material is stored on a UNIX system you may simply need to place it in a suitably named directory (often /pub for public) and set the file permissions so that anyone can read its contents, but not write or execute them. Make sure that all the rest of your filestore is secure – ask your institution's IT service for advice.

Alternatively, you may have to copy the files to a special directory which holds all the files available by anonymous ftp from your site. Your files will probably be stored together in a sub-directory for convenience.
You may be free to make any materials you wish available, or your institution may have a stringent Internet access control policy and will insist that they are checked and centrally managed.

Personal ftp

If you just want to make material available to colleagues, you can give them your username and password so that they can log on to your account and copy the files they need. You obviously have to trust them not to pry or accidentally delete files. You can arrange temporary access of this sort quickly by phone or email and you can change your password once they have got what they needed.

Note that your institution's IT service may insist that you do not allow anyone else log on to your account under any circumstances.

Gopher

You will need to talk to the person who maintains the Gopher site to ensure that the menus are edited to include options which link to your material, and also to ask where you must store the materials.

World Wide Web

Most institutions allow departments to create Web pages which can be accessed either via a central Web server or on their own Web server. Some institutions also allow individuals to create their own Web pages and make materials held in a specific directory (such as `/public_html`) of their UNIX account available via a Web server. There will be a document which defines what your institution regards as acceptable use – rules and guidelines on what you may and may not publish.

Materials stored or created on a PC will need to be transferred to the UNIX filestore by ftp. In general, text documents need to be in HTML format and images in GIF format.

Technology in Teaching   5   Using the World Wide Web

4   Communicating using computers

This chapter gives information about using computers to communicate with individuals and groups. The main technologies discussed are:

▲ Electronic mail (email), which is used for the exchange of messages between individuals anywhere in the world.

▲ Mailing lists, which use email to create a forum for discussion, collaboration and co-operation between groups of people who choose to join. They can be used for a range of activities, from holding electronic meetings to registering for conferences.

▲ Usenet, an Internet service which allows people to create, read and contribute to international, special-interest discussion groups, ranging from serious topics to bizarre beliefs and trivial gossip.

▲ Computer conferencing, which enables small groups of people to hold discussions by leaving messages on a computer system. Individual members of the group can access the system at a time convenient to them in order to read and reply to messages. Computer conferencing is widely used to support learning.

▲ Video conferencing, which allows small groups of people to hold discussions in real time. They can see and hear each other, and may also be able to share data or otherwise collaborate using computer software.

4.1   *Electronic mail*

Electronic mail (often shortened to email or e-mail):
- enables you to send and receive written communications to other computer users conveniently and quickly
- combines the speed, convenience and informality of a telephone call with the assurance of delivery and the permanence of a letter
- can deliver messages within minutes – even to computers on the other side of the world
- often works out cheaper than using traditional mail methods to send messages, which usually have to be typed and/or printed, then put in an envelope, stamped and posted.

Because it is relatively slow in comparison with electronic mail, normal mail is often called 'snailmail' by email users

Handling messages using email also has advantages over traditional methods. For example:
- incoming messages can be stored until you are ready to deal with them
- it is easy to reply to messages or forward them to others
- messages can be saved and grouped in folders for ease of reference
- unwanted messages can be deleted at the push of a button, and without wasting paper.

4.1.1 Mail servers

Most sites have mail server software which helps users to create, read, process and store their email using a simple text-only interface. A terminal emulator is used to communicate to the mail server by sending it the commands you type and displaying its output on your PC's screen. You have to log on to the mail server using your username and password, which ensures that no one else can access your email messages. Software for UNIX systems includes Elm and Pine.

Any PC which can access the mail server can be used to read and send email.

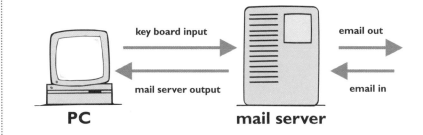

A simple text-based interface is used to manage email. Here a Windows terminal emulator (Telnet) has been used to log on to the mail server (Elm).
This is a list of email messages waiting to be dealt with.

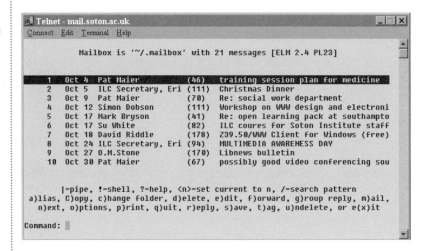

You can read a
message simply
by selecting it
from the list. You
can then delete
it, send a reply,
save it for future
reference or
forward it to
someone else.

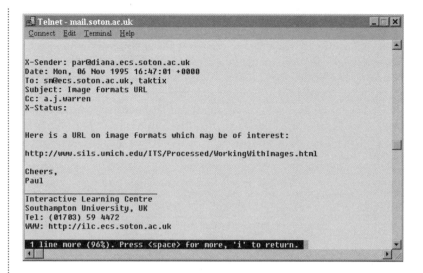

```
Telnet - mail.soton.ac.uk                              _ □ ×
Connect   Edit   Terminal   Help

X-Sender: par@diana.ecs.soton.ac.uk
Date: Mon, 06 Nov 1995 16:47:01 +0000
To: sm@ecs.soton.ac.uk, taktix
Subject: Image formats URL
Cc: a.j.warren
X-Status:


Here is a URL on image formats which may be of interest:

http://www.sils.umich.edu/ITS/Processed/WorkingWithImages.html


Cheers,
Paul

Interactive Learning Centre
Southampton University, UK
Tel: (01703) 59 4472
WWW: http://ilc.ecs.soton.ac.uk

1 line more (96%). Press <space> for more, 'i' to return.
```

The advantages of this system include the following:

▲ users can access their email from any computer with terminal emulation software and access to the mail server: this is particularly useful for users who do not have their own networked PC

▲ email can be accessed from any networked site by connecting to the relevant mail server across the network

▲ users can access their email from home via a modem and telephone line (provided remote access is supported by the mail server)

▲ terminal emulators are available for all types of computers: the mail server's user interface is the same whatever type of computer is used to access it

▲ the speed, memory, storage and display of local computers are not significant factors, as long as standard terminal emulation software is available (this means that otherwise 'obsolete' computers can still have a use)

▲ the mail server stores messages and keeps backup copies in case of hardware failure.

The disadvantages are:

▲ you need to learn how to use a UNIX text editor: if you are used to modern user-friendly interfaces, you may find this unattractive and difficult to use

▲ copying text between word-processed files stored on the PC and email messages can sometimes be a fairly complicated process.

4.1.2   *Mail clients*

Mail client software run on your Windows PC or Apple Macintosh provides a user-friendly interface to the mail server and helps to integrate email with other software. In use, the mail client logs on to the mail server, automatically copies any new messages to your PC's hard disk and then logs off. The messages can then be read, deleted or stored as required. Messages and replies can be prepared using either the built-in text-editor or by pasting in text from a word processor. When you have finished, the mail client logs on to the mail server again, transmits your messages and logs off.

The mail server stores your email until you log on. The mail client then copies it to your PC so that you can read and manage it.

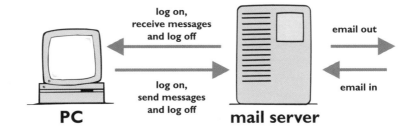

The mail client (in this case, Eudora) displays a list of email messages waiting to be dealt with.

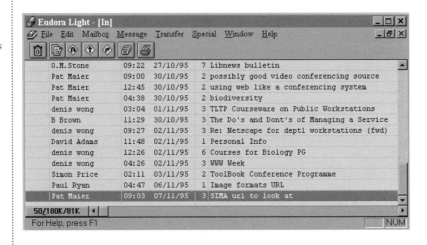

You can read a message by selecting it from the list.

You can then delete it, send a reply, save it on your hard disk for future reference or forward it to someone else.

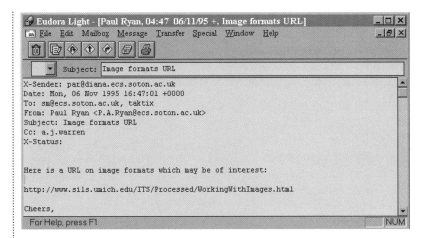

The client–server arrangement has a number of advantages:

▲ it minimizes the time taken to connect to the mail server – if you use a modem and telephone line or a commercial mail service charging by the minute, this will help to keep running costs down

▲ the modern graphical user interface which operates the program and processes messages is relatively easy to use

▲ messages can be stored on the local PC and are thus readily accessible for as long as you choose

▲ information in word-processed files can easily be transferred into email messages

▲ mail client software, which can be programmed to log on automatically to the mail server every so often, will download any new messages and alert you to their arrival

▲ some mail servers (those which support MIME – Multipurpose Internet Mail Extensions) allow other data types, such as binary data files, images, sounds or even video, to be embedded in email messages.

4.1.3 *Commercial email services*

All commercial network services offer email facilities as part of their basic package. Their custom software provides a user-friendly interface to the range of services, information and software on offer. A modem and telephone line are needed to connect your PC to the service. Users are charged a basic monthly fee, in return for which they gain a few hours' use of the standard facilities, but this is still the cheapest and most convenient way for those without networked computers to get on-line and use email. Many Internet Service Providers (ISPs) have emerged over the past few years which just offer a relatively low-cost link to the Internet. These use standard mail clients to manage email accounts, and also charge a monthly fee for basic services.

4.1.4   *Accessing email from home*

You can access an email account from home by connecting your PC to the telephone line using a modem: this converts digital signals produced by the PC into analogue sounds carried over telephone lines. At the mail server, another modem converts the sounds back into digital information.

Modems are used to encode and decode the digital data, so that it can be transmitted as sound along the phone line

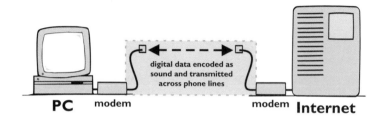

 Technology in Technology   2.5   About modem connections

Such remote access is possible only if the mail server allows dial-up access: as it can pose a security threat, special permission and additional passwords may be needed when logging on to the mail server. Many organizations have more than one modem so that several people can use the mail server (or other computer services) simultaneously.

You will need to experiment to get the modem link working correctly: your institution's IT service should be able to tell you the correct modem settings, and you should be able to save these so that when you next connect to the mail server all you have to do is choose the appropriate name from a menu.

Most modems come with terminal emulator software that will enable you to communicate with the mail server. Alternatively, you may be able to use a mail client across your modem connection; ask your institution's IT service for details. The advantage of this option is that it minimizes connection time, thus not only keeping down your telephone bills but also freeing the mail server's modem and therefore enabling others to use the service.

4.1.5   *Email addresses*

Most email addresses on the Internet take the general structure person@site.domain.
For example:

A.N.Other@soton.ac.uk	the person's initials and last name are used to identify the user
Anna_Other@soton.ac.uk	in this case, the full name is used, but since spaces are not recognized an underscore is used instead
ano195@soton.ac.uk	here the person's computer username identifies him/her
70006.101@compuserve.com	commercial network services may have their own address format.

Note that not all these forms are supported by all sites.

The site name may simply be the 'name' of the organization (such as *soton* for the University of Southampton) or it may include the names of individual departments and/or computer systems (for instance, *ecs.soton* is the email service run by the department of Electronics and Computer Science at the university).

Technology in Teaching   2.3.2   How are computers identified on the Internet?

4.1.6   *Email messages*

Email messages have two basic parts, the header and the body:

▲ the header contains control information: much of this will mean very little to most users, and some email software therefore displays only those parts of the header which are of relevance – namely `From`, `To`, `Date` and `Subject`

▲ the body contains the text of the message. As messages are usually restricted to the 7-bit ASCII character set, many special characters (including the £ sign and foreign language characters and accents) cannot be transmitted.

The header is created by the mail server when a message is transmitted, and it is modified by other systems on the way to its destination. This process can be complicated, as shown by this example:

```
From BADGER@DE.EMBL-Heidelberg Mon Feb  8 16:08:38 1995
Received: from [192.54.41.21] by mail.soton.ac.uk; Mon, 8 Feb
95          15:58:26 GMT
Received: from EMBL-Heidelberg.DE by EMBL-Heidelberg.DE (PMDF
          V4.2-14 #2491)
id <07H52N8BIXROLEEJTG@EMBL-Heidelberg.DE>; Mon, 8 Feb 1995
     12:46:11 +0100
Date: Mon, 08 Feb 1995 12:46:11 +0100
From: Bertie Badger <BADGER@DE.EMBL-Heidelberg>
Subject: Database Advice
To: A.N.Other@uk.ac.southampton.mail
Message-Id: <07H52N8BIXROLEEJTG@EMBL-Heidelberg.DE>
X-Vms-To: ANNA
Mime-Version: 1.0
Content-Type: TEXT/PLAIN; CHARSET=US-ASCII
Content-Transfer-Encoding: 7BIT
Status: OR
```

4.1.7   *Email features and facilities*

Mail server and mail client software have different capabilities and user interfaces, but most offer the following features:

▲ Messages received are displayed as a list showing the sender's name and the subject of the message: this makes it easy to find important messages and delete unwanted ones.

▲ Selecting a message from the list loads it automatically into a viewer so that it can be read.

▲ Messages can be saved to named folders from either the list or the viewer, for future reference and processing. Folders can be created as required.

▲ You can easily reply to a message, attaching the original message (as a whole or quoting selected parts) if necessary: this makes it easy to answer queries point by point. Original messages included in a reply are usually indicated by a > at the start of each line, to differentiate them from your response.

The subject header of a reply message is normally the same as the original but with Re: before it. For example, the reply to a message with the subject header 'Database advice' would be 'Re: Database Advice'.

▲ You can easily forward messages to other people, adding your own comments if you wish.

▲ You can assign a nickname, or alias, to someone you often send messages to, making the email address shorter and easier to type – for instance, *anna* rather than

A.N.Other@soton.ac.uk. Aliases can also be created for groups of people, making it simple to send the same message to everyone in the group.

▲ Many systems allow you to close down your mailbox temporarily – for example, while you are on holiday. Any messages sent to you during this time will return to the originator with a message explaining that you are away.

▲ Many systems enable you to create a signature file: this is attached to the end of all your outgoing messages and should include details such as your name, address and telephone number. Some people also include a disclaimer or a quotation.

4.1.8 *Email conventions and 'netiquette'*

You can add emphasis or expression to your messages by using some widely understood conventions:

▲ _underscores_ are used for emphasis (as bold text is in letters)

▲ *asterisks* are used to highlight (like italics)

▲ CAPITALS are for strong emphasis only (email messages typed entirely or mainly in capitals are widely regarded as shouting!)

▲ 'smileys' are facial expressions created from keyboard characters which are used to indicate the mood or intention of the writer. Some people think they are great, while others consider them trivial. Here are some basic smileys:

:-)	happy
:-(	sad
;-)	wink (in other words, don't take this seriously)

Email tends to be seen as an informal method of communication (like a telephone call), and so is not given as much attention and care as, say, a letter. However, as with letter-writing, there is a form of etiquette ('netiquette'):

▲ Take reasonable care with grammar, spelling and punctuation. Speed may be one of the advantages of email, but it is usually a good idea to read through and, if necessary, correct your message before sending it – a poorly typed message with glaring spelling and grammatical errors will reflect badly on the sender.

▲ Keep messages short and to the point, having consideration for those who have to pay for their email facilities.

▲ Be selective when quoting from other people's messages, particularly if you are replying to a message from a Usenet group or mailing list – others on the list will have seen the original and are unlikely to want to read it all again.

▲ Your signature file should be no more than five lines. If you include a quotation, think about changing it every so often.

4.2   Mailing lists

Mailing lists make it easy for a group of people to share information and hold discussions using email. Any message sent by a member of the group to the mailing list is automatically copied to all other members of the group. Once they have read the message they can:

- delete it if it is of no interest
- respond by emailing the sender direct
- respond by emailing the list, if they believe the rest of the group will be interested in what they have to say.

For example, a member of a mailing list interested in women's studies may post a message asking for details of a book she has heard about. One person who has read the book may email the information direct to the originator, while another may consider it of interest to others on the list and post the details for everyone to read. Other people on the same list might have developed an ongoing 'discussion' through email messages about issues raised in a TV programme about divorce law.

Messages sent to the list are forwarded to everyone else on the list by the mail list server.

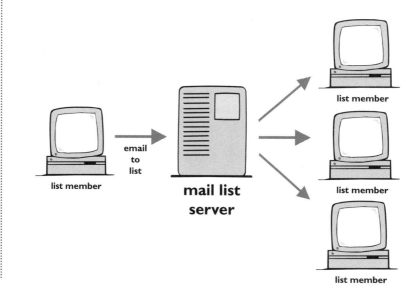

4.2.1   Mailbase: UK academic mailing lists

Mailing lists for the UK academic community use the Mailbase system, which is based at Newcastle University in England. Mailbase enables researchers and academics to communicate and collaborate using electronic mail, and is used in a variety of ways, such as:

- creating self-help discussion groups
- locating and contacting colleagues with similar specialist interests
- holding electronic meetings
- distributing training and teaching materials
- writing and publishing electronic journals and newsletters
- co-authoring papers
- distributing research material and data
- distributing publicity materials
- advertising vacant posts
- registering for conferences.

Other countries also have a wide range of educational mailing lists, although their actual use and membership is often international. For example, the ASKEric site in the US maintains an archive of education Listserv messages at
http://ericir.syr.edu/plweb-cgi/fastweb?searchform+listservs

4.2.2 *Obtaining information on Mailbase by email*

There are three documents which give you all the help you need to start using Mailbase. The first is a directory of the lists available, with short descriptions. The other two are the Mailbase user guide and FAQ (list of frequently-asked questions, with answers). Once you have read these you can decide whether there are any lists you wish to join and send the appropriate commands to Mailbase.

You can use email to obtain these documents by sending a message like this one to *mailbase@mailbase.ac.uk*

```
From: your-email-address
Date: Sat, 16 Dec 1995 13:28:37 PST
Subject: info
To: mailbase@mailbase.ac.uk
lists full
send mailbase user-guide
send mailbase user-faq
stop
```

The Mailbase program will automatically extract your email address and commands from your message and send you the required information as email messages.

4.2.3 *Getting information from the World Wide Web*

Mailbase has a World Wide Web site which gives easy access to all the lists, and has well organized and searchable archives of every lists' messages. Relevant

▲ ▲

documentation and help is also available. This Web site is the best way to make effective use of the information generated by the lists: its Internet address is *http://www.mailbase.ac.uk*

4.2.4   *Being a member of a mailing list*

Once you join a list you will start to receive a fairly steady stream of email messages from its members. Some lists are fairly quiet while others are busy and generate a lot of messages. The 'list owner' and the list members generally ensure that everyone keeps their messages to the point.

If you feel you have something to say, send your email to list_*name@mailbase.ac.uk*. For example:

```
From A.N.Other@soton.ac.uk Fri Dec 15 13:28:05 1995
Date: Mon, 18 Dec 1995 12:43:35 PST
Subject: Re: Mexican Immigration Policy
To: american-studies@mailbase.ac.uk
Dear all,
I disagree with Alex Bourne when he said that
> many studies conclude that the only answer is electronic
> barriers
since this has already been proved by etc. etc.
```

Note the use of selected quotations from the message being replied to. All email programs allow the inclusion of text from an original message in any reply, and you can simply delete the parts you don't want to quote. It is usually better to respond direct to the person sending a message using the reply function of the email program, rather than sending responses to an entire list.

You can keep personal copies of messages you find useful, but also remember Mailbase maintains an archive of all messages. If you have access to the World Wide Web, you can easily search the archives for specific terms, or browse them using the hypermail facility.

Technology in Teaching   4.4.2   Hypermail

Even if you join only one or two popular lists you will probably receive large amounts of email every day. If so, you should read the subject headings and select those messages which seem relevant or of interest to you, deleting the rest without reading them. You can avoid having to plough through several hundred messages when you return from a break by instructing Mailbase to suspend your list memberships until you return.

4.3   Usenet

Usenet is the most controversial Internet service, as it offers a public forum for anyone with Internet access and something to say. Many Usenet newsgroups are trivial or obscure, while others provide an intelligent forum for discussion and enable people to share news and views on academic disciplines and current events without any form of official control. Understandably, many governments – especially those with repressive regimes – are concerned about this new platform for free speech and are taking steps to ensure that their citizens don't have access to it.

Most Usenet newsgroups focus on special interests, such as television programmes, software, religion and hobbies. Such newsgroups are harmless, though the casual observer may find them difficult to understand – many newsgroups have their own 'in' jokes and jargon, and a large number of the messages posted are likely to be short replies to other messages – rather like chatting at a party.

Newsgroups can generate much trivial and often unwanted material. However, some are moderated, which means that all messages are checked by a volunteer before being made generally available. This means that the quality of the information is much higher.

Most academic institutions do not provide access to Usenet because of its controversial nature and also because the JANET (Joint Academic NETwork) regulations explicitly forbid non-academic use of the network and the transmission of offensive material. Some institutions allow restricted access to Usenet newsgroups by, for example, preventing access to .alt (the 'alternative', and most dubious) groups. If you want access to all Usenet newsgroups, you will probably have to use your home computer and subscribe to a commercial Internet service provider.

Technology in Teaching   2.4   How do you get connected?

4.3.1   Newsgroup names

There are around 20,000 Usenet newsgroups, organized using a simple naming convention which enables users to find those of interest. The newsgroup rec.audio.car, for example, is a recreational group (as shown by 'rec') developed as a forum for discussion about audio equipment ('audio') in cars ('car'), while rec.audio.tech is for people interested in hi-fi technology. Similarly, soc.culture.kuwait is a social issues group for people who wish to discuss Kuwaiti culture, and alt.culture.kuwait is an alternative group on the same topic.

The main top-level categories are:

Category	Subject area
alt	alternative – anything goes!
biz	business and commerce
comp	computers and software
misc	miscellaneous – but generally serious
rec	recreations and hobbies
news	discussions about Usenet itself
sci	science and technology
soc	social and cultural issues
uk	UK-related topics

There are many other top-level categories: k12 is for discussions about the US education system, and solent is used by those in the Southampton, Portsmouth and Bournemouth area. Not all categories are available at every site – categories such as solent, for example would be of little interest or use to people living outside the area.

4.3.2 *Newsgroup articles, follow-ups and threads*

Special newsreader software is used to view newsgroups: with this you can see email messages known as articles and, if other people have read those articles and responded, related follow-ups. Together, an article and its follow-ups are known as a discussion thread. The newsreader software displays only the subject line of each article and can hide any follow-ups unless you choose to see them. The text of an article can be viewed by selecting it from the list.

The example below shows some articles from the newsgroup rec.audio.tech. The second article is a thread, having five follow-ups, and three other articles have follow-ups, which are shown by the arrow beside their subject line. The Free Agent software enables follow-ups to be displayed or hidden by clicking on the arrow.

Free Agent is a Windows-type newsreader having three areas in which are displayed a list of available newsgroups, a list of articles in the selected newsgroup, and the text of the selected article.

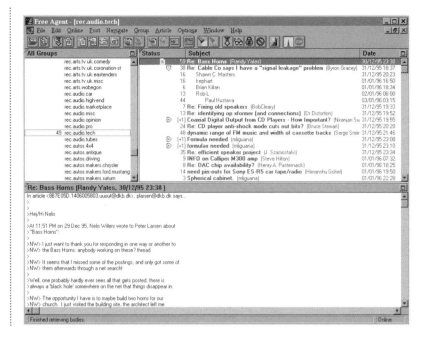

4.3.3 Using Usenet

When you use newsreader software for the first time, it will download and display a list of all the newsgroups available, and this may take a few minutes. Once it has downloaded the details, you can browse through the names to find one that sounds interesting, then sample the articles to find out more. Having found a newsgroup you like and subscribed to it, you can set your newsreader to show articles only from that newsgroup when you connect to your Internet service provider. You can subscribe to as many groups as you wish, and can easily unsubscribe from any newsgroup or browse through the full list again at any time.

Basic newsreader software makes it easy to read, post or follow up articles, and enables you to save articles on disk or email them to others. More sophisticated newsreaders have additional features, such as:

- automatic retrieval of new article subject lines
- automatic retrieval of articles on marked threads
- the ability to create 'kill lists': these automatically ignore articles by a specific author or on a particular subject
- a 'watch list' facility, which automatically retrieves articles by a specific author or on a particular subject
- automatic decoding of articles containing binary information (such as images, sounds or programs).

Off-line newsreaders minimize the amount of time you need to spend connected to the Internet service provider (ISP) and so help to keep costs down. The usual procedure to follow when using this type of software is as follows:

1 connect to your ISP, download new article subject lines and disconnect
2 scan the article subject lines, mark those articles which you wish to read in full
3 connect to the ISP again, download the marked articles and disconnect
4 read the articles, and compose new articles or follow-ups as you wish
5 reconnect to your ISP, upload your articles or follow-ups, and disconnect.

Using an on-line newsreader you stay connected while you download, read and compose articles, and so are likely to incur hefty service charges and telephone bills.

4.3.4 How does Usenet work?

Like the Internet, Usenet does not have any central controlling organization but relies on co-operation between networks and computer systems.

If you write an article and send it to the newsgroup, it is first stored by your ISP's news server, then, at regular intervals (usually daily, but sometimes hourly), the server automatically connects to one or more other news servers in order to exchange new articles. In this way your article is passed from computer to computer across the Internet in a journey that might take a couple of days.

New articles are passed from computer to computer across the Internet.

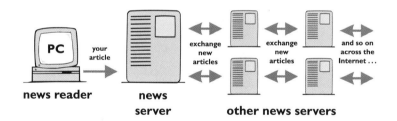

Your ISP's news server can only carry newsgroups available from the news servers it exchanges with, and many sites provide only a restricted 'news feed' – in other words, they do not carry all newsgroups.

It is estimated that about 60 megabytes of articles are created every day. It is clearly impossible for every news server to archive all articles, and so messages more than a few days old are deleted or 'expired'. If you want to keep articles you should store them on your own PC's hard disk.

4.3.5   *Usenet etiquette and jargon*

The first rule which novice Usenet users ('newbies') should heed is to avoid asking stupid questions: most newsgroups post FAQ (frequently-asked questions) articles which deal with the basics. There is also a list of FAQs for all newsgroups in the newsgroup `news.answers`.

It is probably a good idea to 'lurk' in a newsgroup for a week or two – reading articles but not posting any yourself – until you feel more confident, and less of a newbie. You should be prepared to develop a thick skin when you start to post articles, as other members of your newsgroup may disagree with what you write, and will make their views known to you in no uncertain terms. This is known as being 'flamed', and you should not take such disagreement personally – it is better to respond intelligently and politely, enabling other readers of the newsgroup to figure out for themselves who is right, than to start a 'flame war', which can quickly degenerate into personal abuse.

Some newsgroup articles are full of jargon, abbreviations and acronyms (for example TLA, which means a three-letter acronym). There may be a glossary file which explains such terms, but you may find you have to pick things up as you go along. Some of the more common acronyms are:

IMHO	in my humble (or honest) opinion
AFAIK	as far as I know
ROFL	rolls on the floor laughing
FYI	for your information
BTW	by the way.

Your communications with newsgroups should follow the general email conventions and 'netiquette' described. Some people like to adopt an unofficial policing role and will let you know by email if you break any unwritten laws. Such criticism may be useful, but don't take it personally.

Many newsreaders enable articles to be sent to several newsgroups, but you should ensure that the articles you post are relevant to all the newsgroups to which you send them. Sending an article to irrelevant newsgroups is called 'spamming' and is a source of great annoyance to members of Usenet newsgroups.

Technology in Teaching   4.1.8   Email conventions and 'netiquette'

4.4 Computer conferencing

Computer conferencing is often called computer-moderated conferencing, or CMC

Computer conferencing technology enables groups of people to communicate by means of messages on a computer system. Members of the group can access the system at any convenient time to read and reply to messages. It is similar in many respects to the Usenet newsgroups described in Technology 4.3, but membership of these groups is restricted. Through CMC, students and tutors can discuss issues and collaborate on assignments without having to meet physically, and it is therefore often used to support distance learning and can be helpful in overcoming student isolation.

Let us take the example of a tutor who is giving a course about British politics in the 19th century. After training the students in the use of the computer conferencing software, the tutor tells them to log on to the system to find out about their assignment.

Every student has a unique username and password, which are used to control access to the system and as a means of recording usage. The students log on using any PC with a connection to the system (this could be from their own PC at home connected via a modem). They can log on when they find it convenient, but it is a good idea to check for new messages every day.

In our example, a student logging on for the first time will find one message from the tutor giving details of the assignment, and another asking for their views on some aspect of Disraeli's government covered in a recent lecture:

```
assignment
query about Disraeli's government
```

The student's response to this query is used to start a discussion thread: other students will see both the original query and the first student's answer, and will be able to use both as a basis for their responses.

```
assignment
query about Disraeli's government
  answer from first student
  answer from second student
```

Because the discussion is not happening in real time the students have the opportunity to think carefully about their responses and do some background reading before posting their follow-up message. The tutor will also read the thread and may make comments to provoke further discussion.

Students are free to send messages on other topics and so initiate other discussion threads.

```
assignment
query about Disraeli's government
  answer from first student
  answer from second student
  comment from tutor about second student's answer
  response from second student
  answer from third student
a query about the assignment from a student
  answer from tutor
  answer from another student
a query on another topic from a student
```

In this way, computer conferences can stimulate debate between students and the tutor.

The tutor may find he or she has to work hard to keep debates going, and to provide extra encouragement for some students to make a contribution. Email can be used for private communication between students and the tutor outside the public conference. Some computer conferences are organized as a set of 'rooms', where each room is a separate conference. There may be a 'concourse' where general messages are left, a 'library' containing resource materials, a 'coffee bar' for social discussions, and several 'classrooms' where sub-groups of students can collaborate on assignments. For an excellent paper on the educational use of computer conferencing, see this URL: *gopher://ukoln.bath.ac.uk:7070/00/BUBL_Main_Menu/B/BA/BA29_-_Computer_Conferencing_Paper_-_Learning_by_Communicating*

4.4.1 *Computer conferencing software*

All computer conferencing systems run with a server program which stores and organizes the messages. A client program running on the user's PC interacts with the server to display the messages using a modern graphical user interface.

Some older systems did not have client programs, so users had to log on to the server using a terminal emulation program. As the interface was text-based, the system had the advantage that almost any type of computer could be used to access the system, whereas some modern client software is only available for, say, Windows PCs.

There are a number of computer conferencing systems available, such as:

FirstClass, which is a high-performance system integrating email with computer conferencing (often known as groupware in the business world). It also provides powerful tools that use SQL (Structured Query Language) to extract useful information from databases. See this URL for further detailed information: *http://www.wisc.edu/firstclass/*

▲ Servers are available for computers running the Macintosh and Windows NT operating systems.

▲ Clients are available for Macintosh and Windows PCs. VT100 terminal emulator access is also possible from other computers such as UNIX workstations or DOS PCs.

▲ Versions of the FirstClass client are available in 12 languages, including French Canadian, German, Portuguese, Spanish, Japanese and Swedish.

▲ The servers are designed to work directly with modems, enabling the same ease of use, functionality and high performance over network or modem connections.

Lotus Notes is the original groupware application. Notes enables users to use client software to communicate securely over a local area network or telecommunications link, with a document residing on a server. Notes combines an application development environment, a document database and a sophisticated messaging system.

▲ Servers are available for most modern operating systems, including Windows, Windows NT, Novell Netware, OS/2, Solaris, and AIX.

▲ Clients are available for an equally wide range of computers.

▲ Versions of the client and server software are available in most major languages.

▲ **Lotus Notes** has many add-ons available which greatly extend its functionality. See this Internet address for further detailed information: *http://www.lotus.com/home/notes.htm*

Caucus, a dedicated computer conferencing system, has been updated to include a Windows client.

▲ The server runs on a UNIX computer.

▲ Clients are available for Windows PCs. VT100 terminal emulator access is also possible from other computers such as DOS PCs.

▲ For further detailed information contact CECOMM on 01703 714434.

4.4.2 *Hypermail*

Hypermail is a UNIX program which organizes and processes the email messages in a UNIX mailbox to generate a linked set of World Wide Web documents. The messages can be sorted and displayed by subject, date, author or thread. Threads are replies to an original message that form an ongoing discussion; Hypermail uses the `Re: subject` line to recognize these.

Mailbase uses Hypermail to organize its archive of mailing list messages.

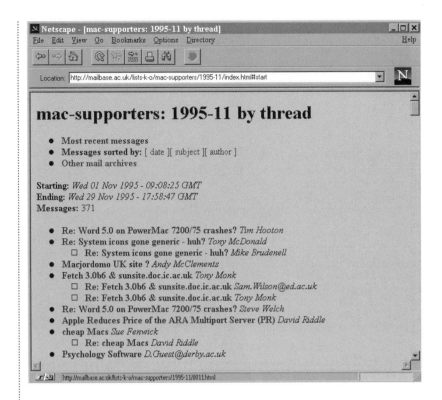

Each message has links to the next and previous messages (by date) and the next message in the thread (if any). Any World Wide Web addresses (URLs) in the messages are turned into links, and email addresses can also be coded so that clicking on them launches an email program with the address already filled in.

This software can be used to create a computer conferencing system which only requires its users to have access to email and a World Wide Web browser. It therefore integrates well with other teaching resources available on the Web and allows students to work in a familiar environment.

The software, available free of charge for non-commercial purposes, is obtainable from Enterprise Integration Technologies at this URL:
http://www.eit.com/software/hypermail/

4.5 Video conferencing

Video conferencing is about real-time communication between people in which the visual element is important. This communication can be between groups of people, as in a meeting or lecture, or between individuals.

4.5.1 Early video conferencing

At first, video conferencing was used by large technological corporations (such as IBM) to enable meetings between executives located around the globe – without their actually having to travel to the meeting. The companies invested in specially-equipped conference studios at their major sites and linked them by satellite during meetings. Video cameras and large screens ensured that the executives could see and speak to each other, and technicians ensured that the cameras 'followed the action'. Needless to say, the whole exercise was very expensive, but it did allow these companies to explore the possibilities offered by the technology.

4.5.2 Video conferencing for groups

More recently, stand-alone units consisting of a camera, large TV screen and special electronics have become available. In an ordinary conference room these are plugged into an ISDN phone line to connect to similar units at remote conference rooms. It is possible to link several sites simultaneously in this way so as to hold 'multi-point' meetings. The cameras are remote-controlled so that they can focus on individuals, flip-charts and so on, but the units usually switch automatically to show whoever is speaking on all the screens. The cost is fairly high but is still less than jetting executives around the globe from one first-class hotel to another!

The market leader (PictureTel) has produced a special podium which can be used by lecturers to show slides, videos, PC screens and printed materials – as well as themselves talking. It can also control units in remote lecture theatres in order to monitor and communicate with the students and create the interactivity which is vital to effective learning. The whole system is controlled using a simple touch-screen which allows the lecturer to concentrate on the teaching rather than the technology.

4.5.3 Desktop video conferencing

Recent developments integrate video conferencing facilities with desktop computers. The basic requirements are a fast, modern PC with a graphical user interface, a sound card and speakers, a video camera, microphone and digitizer card, a communications card (either ISDN or Ethernet) and suitable software. Some systems use a normal ISDN speaker-phone instead of the sound card/speakers/microphone combination. These new PC-based products are not intended for group communication, but allow individuals to see and talk to each other and also – perhaps more importantly – share screens and programs.

Using a system such as PCS-LIVE from ATS Interact, a designer can show ideas to a client, and discuss any changes required. The client and the designer can annotate pictures, graphics and text placed on a 'shared whiteboard'. It is even possible to control software running on one PC from the other – although the response is still rather slow.

Software-only solutions, such as Intel's ProShare, are now available that allow two networked PCs to share, view and annotate documents while their users talk using standard telephones.

4.5.4 *Why use video conferencing?*

Video conferencing does offer some unique educational possibilities, but these have to be weighed against the costs involved in setting up and running the systems. Video conferencing can be used to provide live, interactive, distance learning for groups of people. Training can be provided to large numbers of students – although the larger the audience, the less interactive the training becomes. Typical benefits include:

▲ Extending the reach of an educational centre, allowing students to participate without having to travel long distances, which is especially important for students who live in remote areas. This factor will also grow in importance as institutions start to market their courses to fee-paying students using worldwide data networks.

▲ Increased quality of education – for example by enabling contributions from leading academics, experts or public figures without requiring them and the students to travel to the same location.

The key word above is *interactive* – otherwise the training could be delivered more easily and far more economically by using video tapes or multimedia CD-ROM.

Desktop video conferencing can be used to provide one-to-one tuition at a distance. It may therefore have a role to play in supporting students of more conventional distance-learning programs by enhancing their contact with tutors. Here are some points to consider:

▲ Moving video images of the participants are not usually critical, in which case less equipment is required and cheaper communication links are possible. With products like Intel's ProShare, all that is required is a Windows PC, a modem and a phone line.

▲ If video images of the participants are required, the current realities of video data and communication speeds mean that the images are quite small and rather jerky.

▲ The technology is still at an early stage of development but will probably soon become as common as using a telephone, email and fax.

▲ The technology to hold multi-point conferences between small groups of individuals is under development – and will greatly enhance the educational potential when it becomes available.

Further information on video conferencing from the *Support Initiative for Multimedia Applications* can be found at this URL: *http://info.mcc.ac.uk/CGU/SIMA/simapj.html*

5 Using the World Wide Web

This chapter is an introduction to one of the most exciting developments in information technology: the World Wide Web. It provides down-to-earth explanations of:

▲ The World Wide Web: what it is and how it works, including screen snapshots showing a typical search for information

▲ Web browsers: the software used to retrieve and display information from the Web

▲ Searching for information: tools and techniques that help you find the information you are looking for

▲ Publishing information: a step-by-step guide to creating your own information resources on the Web

▲ HTML: the HyperText Markup Language used to code Web documents

▲ Web issues: the legal, technical and commercial issues raised by this global information network, plus a look at how the Web is developing.

5.1 *What is the World Wide Web?*

The World Wide Web (often written as WWW, W3 or called simply 'the Web') is a truly global information system that enables you to find, retrieve and view documents stored on computer systems connected to the Internet. It does not require any technical expertise and is so easy to use that almost anyone can pick up the basics in just a few minutes. Its development sparked an explosion in the use and popularity of the Internet.

The Web uses a hypermedia technology that enables links to be made between documents. Links are shown as highlighted text or graphics, and selecting and following a link is as simple as pointing and clicking with your mouse. When you follow a link the linked document is automatically retrieved and displayed. Links can be made between documents stored on systems anywhere on the Internet.

Web documents are usually referred to as web pages. Web pages can contain text, data or digitized images, sound or video. Special software – called a Web browser or navigator – is used to follow links, retrieve pages and display them on the screen. Text appears correctly formatted with features such as headings, bulleted lists and tables. Text and graphics can be mixed on a page.

The following sequence of screen-grabs shows an example World Wide Web session, hopefully giving you a flavour of how it works. Suppose you were interested in classical music and have been listening to works by the English composer Henry Purcell. You hear on the radio that a manuscript containing new works by him has been discovered – can you find anything about this on the Web?

Your first step might be to connect to Lycos, a vast database containing details of nearly all Web documents!

This Web page has a fill-in form so that you can enter the keywords that you are searching for – in this case 'Henry Purcell'.

Lycos sells advertising space so that it can afford to provide a free service to everyone.

A few seconds after clicking on the Search button, the database returns this list of documents, sorted in order of potential relevance.

Each entry has a brief abstract to help you decide whether it is useful. The underlined words are links – clicking on a link retrieves and displays the actual document.

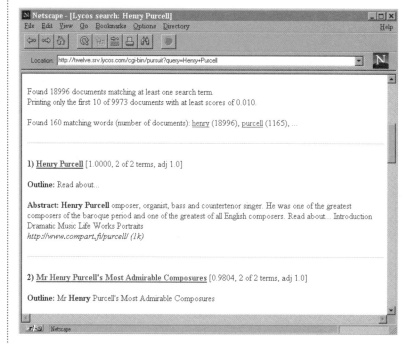

At this stage you would probably follow some of the links and take a look at the documents. The first link is to a short general biography, the second is to a record company's description of a CD recording.

Scrolling down the page you discover that the tenth link is to a page at the British Library's Web site – and you decide to take a look.

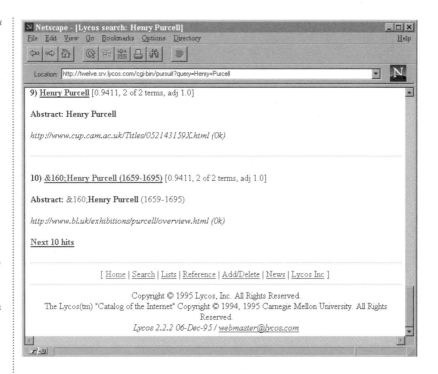

The page starts with an in-line graphic showing Henry Purcell and details of an exhibition about him at the British Library.

This facility to mix text and graphics is one of the Web's great strengths.

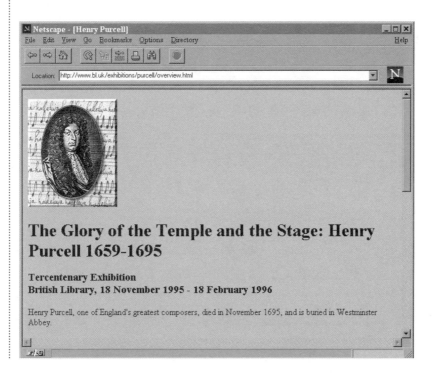

Scrolling down the page you discover more details and some links to other pages – one of which is about the newly-discovered manuscript. Click on the link to follow it!

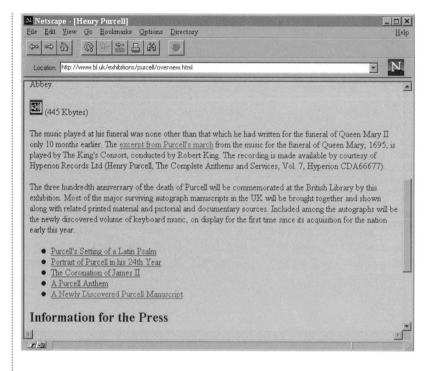

The page starts with an image showing one of the manuscript pages.

Large images like this one can take a minute or so to download if the Internet is busy or if you are using a modem rather than a direct connection.

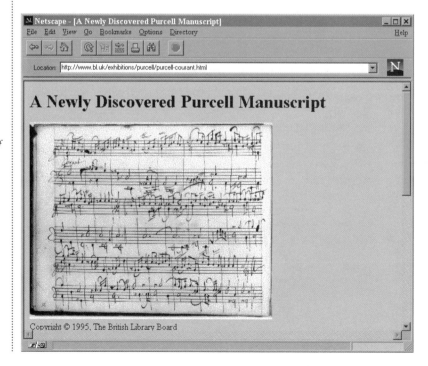

Scrolling down reveals some details about how the manuscript was found and what it contains. Clicking on the audio button (near the top of the page) downloads and plays some (digitized) music from the manuscript (note the audio player's controls).

Perhaps it's worth taking a trip to London to see the exhibition and the manuscript for yourself!

There is a link at the end of each page to the British Library's 'home page' – and from there we can quickly find out the opening hours and location of the exhibition.

Almost all Web sites have a home page which provides an overview of (and links to) the resources available.

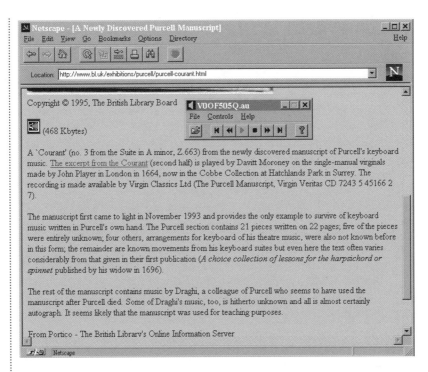

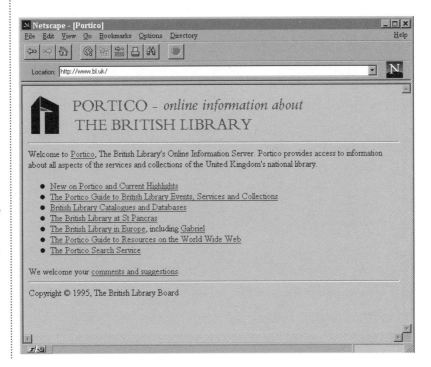

5.2   *How the World Wide Web is spun*

There are two key ideas that make the World Wide Web work:

▲ Web pages are coded ('marked up') to identify the structural elements of the document. These codes are not displayed by the Web browser, but are used to control the appearance of the page on screen. For example, text marked as a title will usually be displayed using a large bold font. The set of rules that define how pages are marked up is called HTML (HyperText Markup Language).

▲ Every Web page has a unique address, called a URL (Uniform Resource Locator). The URL identifies the document type, Internet location and filename.

It is a combination of these two factors – HTML coding and unique URLs – that gives the World Wide Web its unique flexibility, power and ease of use.

▲ HTML enables plain text files to include many advanced features such as lists, tables, fill-in forms, embedded images and links to other files. HTML is extensible since new codes can be defined – for example a code that allows the text colour to be defined. Of course, updated versions of Web browsers are required to understand these codes and display the document correctly.

▲ URLs make it simple to define a link from one Web page to another using a simple HTML code. This has made it easy for authors to create Web pages which include links to other relevant information on Internet servers anywhere in the world. This tangled mass of linked resources is the World Wide Web.

Links can be made from text or images to other Web pages. Links can also be made to other Internet resources, such as ftp archives, Gopher menus and even Telnet connections.

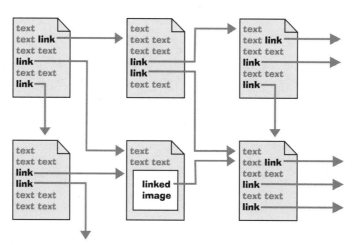

hypertext links between HTML documents

The World Wide Web is based on the interaction between Web browser software running on your PC and Web servers running on remote computers. Here's what happens when you click on a link in a Web page:

1 your Web browser reads the hidden HTML code that gives the URL of the document associated with that link
2 your Web browser sends a request across the Internet to the appropriate web-server computer
3 the Web server receives the message and sends the file requested back to your computer
4 your Web browser interprets the HTML codes and displays the document.

The web browser and server communicate across the Internet using the HTTP protocol.

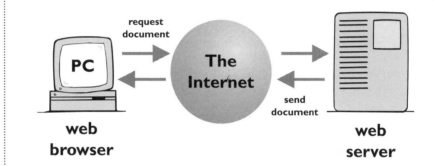

The Web browser communicates with Web servers using an Internet protocol called HTTP (HyperText Transport Protocol). This is why the URL of all Web pages starts with the code *http://*

Web browsers can also communicate with other types of remote server using the appropriate Internet protocol. This allows them to provide a consistent user interface to other Internet services such as ftp (file transfer), telnet (remote access) and Gopher. The latest versions of some browsers also integrate Usenet news and even email. This has unified the previously fragmented Internet services into a coherent whole and largely eliminated the need for an array of separate programs.

All URLs specify which protocol is needed to transfer the file, and you will probably see URLs that start with these codes:

*It has been suggested that the correct English pronunciation of http:// is **hotpotato**!*

http://	HyperText Transport Protocol
ftp://	File Transfer Protocol
telnet://	Telnet remote access
gopher://	Gopher

5.3   Web browsers

When a Web browser displays a Web page it uses the HTML codes to format the document correctly – for example headings usually appear bold and use a larger font than the text. If you re-size the browser's window the page is automatically re-formatted to fit, so text is not lost off the 'edge of the page'. However, some features such as tables may have fixed widths and will not appear correctly if the browser has a narrow window.

Web browser software, such as NCSA Mosaic, Netscape Navigator or Microsoft Internet Explorer, is available for most modern computers and operating systems. This means that Web pages are platform-independent – in other words they should (theoretically) appear the same no matter what computer system is being used to view them.

In practice, of course, there are differences – especially since the Web is still in a period of rapid growth, which means that new features and capabilities are being added all the time. Newer features such as fill-in forms are not supported by older Web browsers and some advanced features such as embedded animations require extra software which is only available for some operating systems. In addition, some Web browsers, notably Netscape and Microsoft Internet Explorer, have their own proprietary HTML codes and capabilities.

An Internet working party is working to define an HTML standard. The current standard is HTML 3.2. Commercial companies like Netscape and Microsoft rely on maintaining their competitive edge and will probably continue to define proprietary codes which are supported only by their Web browser software.

It seems inevitable that, whatever Web browser you have, you will not be able to use all the new features available. The good news is that the HTML standard defines a solid core of basic features supported by most browsers and displayed by them in the same way. To take advantage of new features, you should always upgrade your browser to the latest official version. Some programs are made available for testing as pre-release 'beta' versions, but these can be prone to crashes so use them at your own risk! We recommend that you use the latest version of Netscape Navigator or Microsoft Internet Explorer.

5.3.1   Text-only Web browsers

Although most browsers make good use of a graphical user interface (GUI) to display documents and select options, text-only browsers (such as Lynx) are available. These can be used to access the Web from older computers (eg DOS PCs) or via terminal emulation (eg a modem connection to your UNIX account). While not being able to see any graphics may seem like a disadvantage, the reduction in the amount of data transmitted means faster response times! You can simulate this on other Web browsers by turning off the automatic retrieval of images.

The Lynx Web browser uses the keyboard to select options and follow links.

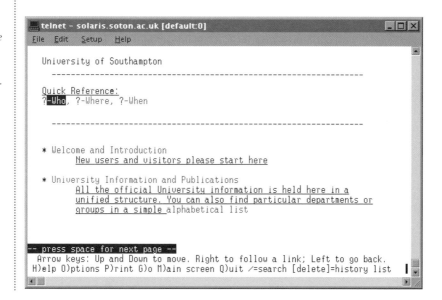

5.3.2 Browser features

Most Web browsers have common features which make it easy and convenient for you to use the World Wide Web.

File menu

The **Open**… option allows you to open a HTML file stored on your PC's hard disk so that you can see how Web pages you are creating will look before you copy them to a Web server. In most cases, you can also check whether any links from the page work.

The **Save As**… option allows you to save the current Web page to your PC's hard disk. You can either save just the text (a .TXT file) or the text with HTML codes (a .HTM file). This allows you to do three things:

1 Store, edit and merge information found on the Web. All word processors can load .TXT text files.

2 Keep copies of useful Web pages on your PC, complete with links that work, so that you always have fast access to them. Keeping the results from an Internet database query is another typical use. Note that any graphics on the page will not be saved. Use the **File Open** option to reload these pages into your browser.

3 Some people find it helpful to copy Web pages that they like so that they can study (and copy!) the HTML code used. This is a good way of learning the subtleties of HTML. However, bear in mind the potential copyright implications of this.

| Technology in Teaching | 5.7.1 | Legal aspects |
| Using Technology | 1.3 | Copyright and intellectual property rights |

The **Print**… option enables you to get a printed version of the current Web page, including graphics. The information will be re-formatted to fit on the paper.

Netscape also has a **New Window** option that enables you to start a second (and third, and fourth) copy of the program. This means that you can view up to four Web pages at once and can get on with browsing and searches while other pages are being (slowly) retrieved.

Edit menu

The **Copy** option allows you to copy selected text from a Web page to the clipboard so that it can be pasted into other documents. If you are doing research using the Web you can easily grab relevant information from the resources you find and compile them into notes. Note that you copy the text only and not the HTML codes.

You can also select and copy the URL of the Web page from the **Location** or **Address** bar to the clipboard so that you can paste it into your notes as a 'reference' for the information gathered.

The **Find** option allows you to search the current Web page for specific text. This works the same way as the Find option in word processors and is particularly useful when searching for items in long lists.

Navigation options

All browsers have toolbar buttons and equivalent menu options that make navigating the Web easier. To speed things up, most browsers save copies of all the Web pages retrieved in a session to a cache in the PC's memory and also on the PC's hard disk. If you revisit one of these pages, the browser reloads it from the cache rather than retrieving it again from the Internet.

The **History** option displays a list of all the pages visited this session and allows you to revisit any page by selecting it from the list.

The **Back** button and the **Forward** button let you step backwards and forwards through the History list one page at a time.

The **Home** button reloads the Web page that you have chosen as your 'home page'– for example the home page of your institution or department. You can configure your browser to load and display this page every time it is started.

The **Stop** button cancels the retrieval of the current Web page. One common reason for using this button is when the data transfer is so slow that you can't be bothered to wait.

The **Reload** button reloads the current Web page from its Internet server rather than the local cache. There are three reasons you might want to do this, to:
1 try again with a page whose retrieval is incomplete or seems to be taking too long
2 get the latest version of a page whose contents change – some pages such as weather maps are automatically generated by computers using live data
3 see whether changes you make to your own Web pages are OK – so you edit the file, save it, reload, check and then edit again if necessary.

Bookmarks, hotlists and favourites
Bookmarks, hotlists and favourites are all terms used to describe a personalized list of useful Web pages. You can reload and display these pages simply by selecting them from the list. If you come across a page that you would like to visit again, you can easily add its URL and description to the list using a toolbar button or menu command. Some browsers allow you to organize the list into a hierarchy, which makes it easier to manage long lists of pages.

A hierarchical bookmark list in Netscape 1.2

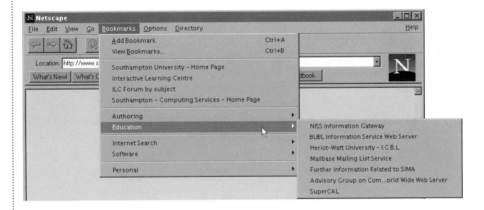

Keeping a hotlist makes the Web much easier to use – you gain one-click access to useful pages such as:
– the home page of your institution and department
– academic information services such as NISS (National Information on Software and Services)
– software archives such as SunSite at Imperial College
– Internet search engines such as Lycos
– Web directories such as Yahoo!

Technology in Teaching   5.4.2   Internet directories

You will often come across interesting information and links while using the Web, and the hotlist is an ideal way of making a note of these. It is often very difficult to 'retrace your steps' and remember how you found the page if you do not make a note – **at the time**! The alternative is to write down the URL in a notebook (not on a scrap of paper…) but this is less convenient and not recommended unless you always have to use public access PCs and so cannot save URLs to the hotlist.

Other options

Most Web browsers allow you to switch off the automatic loading of images on pages. This can greatly speed up the browsing process since less data has to be transferred across the Internet. If you need or want to see the images on a page, there is usually a menu option or toolbar button that will load the images for that page only.

Web browsers usually show links to other URLs in one colour (eg blue) but change the colour (eg to purple) once you have followed the link. This makes it easy to see which links you have followed and which links you haven't. The browser keeps a record of which URLs you have used, so a link to the same URL from another page will also be shown as 'followed'. You can set an 'expiry date' so that they revert to the basic colour after a chosen period (such as 14 days).

Helper applications

Web browsers can be configured to use other software as 'helper applications' to view unsupported file types. Here are three common examples:

▲ Most browsers can display images stored using the GIF format. If you download an image stored in another format (such as JPEG or TIFF) you can set up your browser so that it automatically launches an image editor such as PaintShop Pro or Adobe Photoshop and loads the file so that you can view it.

▲ Digital video files stored in Windows AVI, QuickTime or MPEG formats can only be viewed using additional software. Some browsers can play sound files stored in specific formats (.AU, .AIF), but unsupported formats (such as Windows .WAV) will also need additional software.

▲ Software and data archives usually store their files in a compressed format. This saves space and reduces transmission times. You can set up your browser to launch a utility program that automatically decompresses these files when you retrieve them.

The configuration process is fairly easy – you choose the data type (eg audio/wav), from a list and specify the filename and location of the software used to view it (eg `c:\windows\sndrec32.exe`). Remote access to Internet computers requires Telnet terminal emulation software. Before you can follow links to URLs that begin *telnet://* you have to enter the filename and location of your Telnet software.

Technology in Teaching   3.8   Using Telnet to communicate with remote computers

5.4   *Searching for information on the Web*

The popular image of the World Wide Web is that it is easy to use – and it is true that 'surfing the Internet' by following links between Web pages is simple and fun. However, the sheer volume of material publicly available (around 85 million documents in July 1997) can make finding specific information quickly a problem – unless you know how to search the Internet effectively. The problem is compounded because the material is:

- dynamic – it is constantly being added to, deleted, updated or moved. You cannot rely on finding the same information where you found it last week
- unordered – information about a topic may be found on many different servers, stored in commercial, institutional, departmental or even personal accounts. The information on these servers is not stored in a structured way
- unchecked – anyone can publish information on the Web without peer review. You should cross-check with other sources and consider the reputation or qualifications of the person or organization publishing the information
- uneven – there may be a great deal of up-to-date information available on some topics (especially computer-related topics like virtual reality) but almost nothing on other subjects (for example 'baked beans').

There are three basic ways to search the Internet for information: browsing, Internet directories and Internet search tools.

5.4.1   *Browsing the Web*

Browsing the Web is simple and can be good fun. Its good points are that you can unexpectedly find useful resources that you didn't know existed and weren't even looking for. Its bad points are its random approach and the amount of time you can waste viewing irrelevant (if interesting) material.

Here are some tips for making browsing easier and more useful:

▲ Pick a good starting point. For example, the home page of an agricultural college would be suitable if you were looking for information on organic farming.

▲ Follow your nose. Follow potentially useful links from the start point – if you seem to be getting somewhere, keep following links. If not, retrace your steps and try another option.

▲ Use the **Back** button and the **History** list to retrace your steps quickly if necessary

▲ Switch off graphics. Text-only pages transfer faster, speeding up the whole browsing process.

▲ Avoid peak times if possible. In the UK this means any time when America is awake – so things start to slow down around lunchtime. This obviously does not apply so much when you are browsing European resources.

▲ Make a note of interesting URLs in a notebook or browser hotlist when you find them. Don't put this off, since later you probably won't be able to remember where you found them.

▲ Stick to the task in hand and don't get distracted. If you find interesting but irrelevant material, make a note of its whereabouts but move on quickly.

5.4.2 *Internet directories*

Internet directories are a good place to start when you are looking for information about a broad subject area. They are organized using a logical subject tree so that it is fairly simple to find what you require. For example, here is the top-level of Yahoo! – one of the most popular Internet directories:

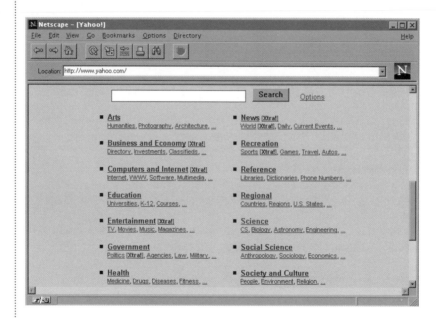

Suppose you are searching for information on organic farming.

1 Clicking on **Science** takes you to a page listing scientific disciplines, one of which is agriculture.

2 Clicking on **Agriculture** displays a page listing agricultural topics, including organic farming.

3 Clicking on **Organic Farming** displays a page containing links to relevant Web pages. These should provide good starting points for further browsing.

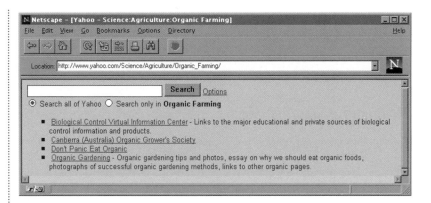

It is often more efficient to type in your query and click on the Search button –
although not all Internet directories have a search feature.

Internet directories are good because the Web pages they index have been suggested
and checked by people, implying that they are useful and have been correctly
categorized. Their disadvantage is that they typically index less than 1% of the Web,
and so are very incomplete. Paradoxically, this limited choice may be an advantage if
you are just looking for a few good starting points for further searches.

Some Internet directories are commercial services that provide a free service by
relying on advertising. The advantage of Web adverts is that you only have to see
them if you want to – and that advertisers make a real effort to make them attractive
and informative.

Here are the URLs of some of Internet directories:

Yahoo!
http://www.yahoo.com/

Clearinghouse
http://www.lib.umich.edu/chouse

There are also useful UK academic sites:

NISS - National Information on Software and Services
http://www.niss.ac.uk
Useful links to UK academic information, subject tree with search facilities, news,
jobs, reference works

BUBL - Bulletin Board for Libraries
http://www.bubl.bath.ac.uk/BUBL/home.html
Useful links to international resources and services, subject tree with search
facilities

See these URLs for more comprehensive lists of Internet directories and search tools:

▲ *http://www.bubl.bath.ac.uk/BUBL/Key.html*

▲ *http://src.doc.ic.ac.uk/cusi/cusi.html*

▲ *http://www.yahoo.com/Computers_and_Internet/World_Wide_Web/Searching_the_Web/*

5.4.3   *Internet search tools*

Internet search tools are the best choice when you are looking for specific information. They work best when you can enter several keywords that tightly focus your query. As an example, a search of the Lycos database for documents containing the word 'organic' found 12,769 items, 'farming' found 4327 items and 'organic farming' only 41 items. Among these 41 items were a few important Web sites not included in the Yahoo directory.

Here is a typical Lycos entry showing abstract information. The underlined document title (agAccess) is a link to that resource.

```
9) agAccess [0.9366, 2 of 2 terms, adj 1.0]
Abstract: agAccess: Agricultural Clearinghouse Please email
questions, comments and additions to agAccess Last Updated
11/15/95 Contents -- Click to move directly to: * International
Sources for Agricultural Information * U.S. Government Sources *
University Sources * Sustainable Agriculture Information *
Sustainable Agriculture Events * Agricultural & Related
Organizations * Organic Farming and Permaculture Information *
Urban Agriculture * Internet Agriculture Guides, Mailing Lists
and Searching Tools International Sources for Agricultural
Information * International Agriculture Sites An assorted mix of
international agriculture sites maintained by the Consolidated
Farm Service Agency (USDA). * USDA
http://www.mother.com/agaccess/Aglinks.html (18k)
```

With most Internet search tools it is possible to specify sophisticated search criteria. For example, you could search for all items about 'A and (B or C) but not D'. The advantage of Internet search tools is that some of them (Lycos and Alta Vista) have very comprehensive databases, so you can be sure of finding most of what is available on the Internet. On the other hand, their very size makes it difficult for them to remain up to date – given the explosive growth of the Web.

Unless you specify your search query carefully, you may find a vast number of barely relevant links. It is also not possible to search for very short words – for example it is simply not possible to find information on the Japanese game of Go by searching for 'go'. In cases like this you will have to think of alternative queries – for example searching for 'Meijin' (a term used to describe an expert Go player) will inevitably find Web pages associated with Go.

It is often a good idea to make several queries using alternative keywords to ensure that you find most of the resources available – owing to the dynamic nature of the Web and the impossibility of making the database complete and up to date, it is never possible to find everything. In some cases you may also need to try alternative spellings – Sarayevo and Sarajevo, for instance.

To summarize, here are some recommendations about Internet search tools and their use:

▲ always make your queries as specific as possible

▲ read the on-line help files to learn how to specify complex queries

▲ if you want a really thorough search, make several queries using alternative terms and spellings

▲ try to avoid peak times (after lunchtime in the UK) if you want a fast response from these US-based services

▲ switch off graphics to speed up transfer times and avoid seeing advertisements.

Here are the URLs of the major Internet search tools:

Lycos   *http://www.lycos.com*

Simple or complex searches possible. Also includes hotlists of the most popular sites in specific areas such as education, entertainment, science, etc.

Alta Vista   *http://www.altavista.digital.com*

Simple or complex searches possible. Also maintains a searchable full-text index of all Web pages and Usenet newsgroups and can find pages containing links to a specified page!

5.5 Publishing information on the Web

Publishing your own Web documents is relatively easy and involves the following basic steps:

▲ plan your Web pages. What are they about? How are they linked?

▲ create and assemble the text, graphics and images

▲ convert these resources into digital files – ASCII text or GIF images – and store them on your PC

▲ mark up the text using HTML codes using a word processor or special HTML editor

▲ check these Web pages using a browser and edit if necessary

▲ copy the files to a directory on a server which is permanently connected to the Internet – this may be the Web server system itself, or another server which is accessible by the Web server

▲ recheck the Web pages on the server; check all the links to resources at other Web sites; edit if required

▲ publicize your new Web pages so that people know they exist and can find them

▲ think how you can improve your Web pages – remember that the Web is a dynamic publishing medium.

The rest of this section looks at these steps in more detail.

5.5.1 Planning your Web pages

Thinking about the answers to these questions will help you plan your Web pages:

▲ Are you able to create your own Web pages? Is it allowed by your organization? Are the facilities and expertise available? Can you get help and advice?

▲ Who is the target audience for these pages? Your students? Your colleagues? Your organization? The rest of the world?

▲ What information will you provide? Administrative? Student assignments? Links to useful resources? Course support materials? Teaching material? Research reports? A general introduction to a subject? Personal interest?

▲ How much time do you want to assign to this task?

In general, it is a good idea to start with a simple and tightly focused idea – and do it quickly and well. Avoid the temptation to take on too much at first, since creating and assembling the resources can be a major task in itself. Because the Web is a dynamic publishing medium, you can easily extend the scope of your Web pages when the need arises and time allows. The Web publishing process will naturally get faster as you gain experience. Beware of spending too much time getting your pages absolutely perfect.

Take at look at the Web pages produced by other departments and sites – use ideas you like and learn from those you don't like. You can view and copy their HTML code to incorporate in your own Web pages.

Nearly all sites have a 'home page' which provides links to the major resources and services offered by that site. The home page should be attractive and short – people want to move on quickly to the areas they are really interested in. Keep any graphics small and non-essential – many people browse with graphics turned off. Don't rely on browser-specific features such as Netscape frames.

5.5.2 *Assembling your resources*

This stage can take a lot of time and effort since it may be equivalent to producing a booklet or even a book! You will probably have to:

▲ write new text using your word processor

▲ word-process old printed or written documents. You may be able to avoid re-typing old printed or typed documents by scanning them and using OCR (optical character recognition) software to turn them into word-processor files

▲ find diagrams, illustrations and photos

▲ create new diagrams, illustrations and photos: diagrams and charts can be re-drawn using graphics, presentation or spreadsheet software.

You should pay close attention to copyright at this stage. While it may be acceptable to photocopy a few pages or diagrams from a textbook as course handouts, publishing that information on the Web is a different matter. You will have to obtain copyright clearance, paraphrase text and recreate graphics to remain within the law.

5.5.3 *Converting to digital files*

All of your resources will have to be stored as computer files:

▲ Some resources, such as word-processed text, will already be stored on your PC.

▲ Photos and diagrams will also need to be scanned and stored as computer files.

Text file formats
All word processors store documents using their own file format, but are capable of saving them in other file formats. Web pages use the simplest text file format, known as plain text or ASCII, which is understood by all word processors and all types of computer.

Text file names
Web servers expect Web pages to have a filename of the format `filename.html` or `filename.htm`, but it is easier to standardize on .htm if you use a DOS or Windows

PC to create the resources. Do not use spaces or non-standard characters in the filename, even on systems such as UNIX, Macintosh or Windows 95 which support long filenames.

Graphics file formats

Images on the Web have to be stored as GIF (Graphics Interchange Format) files. Some newer Web browsers can also display images stored using the more efficient JPEG format – but you can't yet rely on people being able to view these images. Software is available that can translate images files from one format to another, so if your spreadsheet charts are stored as TIFF images you can easily convert them to GIF images.

Graphics file considerations

Image files should not be too large, otherwise they will take a long time to transfer and will not fit on the screen once they have transferred. A good rule of thumb is to avoid images greater than 600 pixels (dots) wide or 400 pixels high. Most images should be less than 300 x 200 pixels. If you are scanning photos or diagrams, your scanner software should allow you to adjust the final size of the image (in pixels) independently of the size of the original.

Organized and safe storage

These resources will have to be stored on your PC's hard disk and records kept so that you can easily see what remains to be done. You might consider using two strategies:
1   Files stored by type – word-processed files in one directory, HTML files in another, GIF files in another and so on.
2   Files stored by task – all files (HTML and GIF) for one purpose in one directory, all files for another purpose in another directory.
Whatever method you choose, retain the same directory structure when copying the files to the Web server – this will simplify linking, checking and updating the files.

Don't forget to keep back-up copies of these files in case of emergencies.

Technology in Teaching   1.10   Backing up your files

5.5.4 *Adding HTML codes to the text*

Web pages are not just plain text files – they also contain special codes which identify structural elements such as headings and lists, or features such as horizontal rules and special characters. Other codes identify links to image files or other Web pages. These codes are specified by HTML, the HyperText Mark-up Language.

These codes are known as tags and are also plain text, so they can be created, viewed and edited using any word processor or text editor. Angle brackets are used to identify tags and they are often used in pairs – a 'start tag' `<tag>` and an 'end tag' `</tag>` – to define the text between them. These tags are not case-sensitive. For example:

`<title> This is the title of the Web page </title>`

You will have to add appropriate tags to all your text files. This can either be done by hand (you type all the tags) or using a special HTML editor which automatically types the tags for you – you just have to show it where you want them.

HTML
Assistant: a text
editor with
special tools to
help you create
Web pages

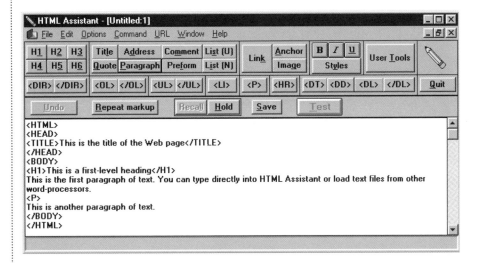

It is also possible to get add-on software for some popular word processors (such as Microsoft Word for Windows, WordPerfect for Windows and ClarisWorks) which also makes it easy to add tags to text files. It seems likely that this will soon become a standard feature of modern word processors.

Internet
Assistant for
Word turns
Word for
Windows into
an HTML editor

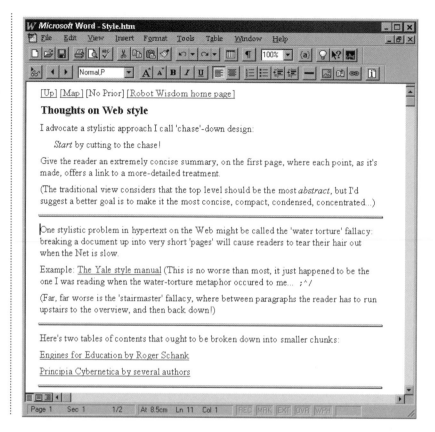

5.5.5   *Transferring files to the server*

When you have created your Web pages and graphics, check them for errors by viewing them with your Web browser – see Technology 5.3.2 for details on how to view files stored on your PC. There are three basic types of mistake:

▲ **Content** Are the text and graphics accurate? Is the text clear? Are the grammar and spelling OK?

▲ **Appearance** Does it look as you planned? Are the HTML codes correct? Are the graphics the right size?

▲ **Links** Do all the links work? You can check all the links between files on your PC, but other links will have to be checked after the files are moved to the server.

Make any corrections that are needed and then check the pages again. Copy the files to the server using a file transfer utility. There may be several things you need to do first:

▲ Talk to your organization's Web site manager and arrange for the files to be copied to an agreed location on the Web server or other computer system. This is probably the most common approach.

▲ Talk to your institution's computing service and find out how to set up your own UNIX account so that it is accessible to the Web server. This is relatively easy, but not all organizations allow it.

▲ Install and configure Web server software on a computer system attached to the Internet. This is a major task and will add significantly to your system manager's workload.

Once the files are on a server you should check them again using a Web browser. Check that all the links work – especially those to external resources. It is a good idea to see how your Web pages look using a variety of browsers – for example, Netscape on a PC, Mosaic on a Macintosh and Lynx on a UNIX system. Some browsers allow bad HTML code while others reject it – and not everyone uses graphical browsers. If you need to correct minor errors you will probably find it easiest to edit the text files on the server. UNIX text editors are fairly primitive (no menus, obscure commands, etc) but do the job efficiently.

5.5.6 *Publicizing your Web pages*

The final step is to announce the existence of your Web pages to your target audience. If these are your students, colleagues, department or institution, this poses few problems – all you need are a few handouts, posters, or an article in a newsletter. If your pages contain academic or specialist resources, you may be able to advertise them through the journals, magazines, mailing lists and meetings of professional bodies.

You can also publicize your work by sending details to the various Internet directories and databases. These services often encourage you to send them your details so that they can be checked and indexed. However, the simplest way to gain publicity for your work is via the Submit-it service (*http://www.submit-it.com*) which copies details to all the Internet directories and search tools.

5.6 *Learning to create Web pages using HTML*

This section looks at the functions and possibilities HTML offers. It is not an HTML tutorial, but if you want to learn to create Web pages using HTML, there are many good tutorials available on the Internet. Here are some URLs:

Vlib: the Web Developer's Virtual Library contains links to all aspects of the World Wide Web: protocols, clients, servers, HTML, etc.
http://WWW.stars.com/Tutorial/HTML/Forms/

A Beginner's Guide to HTML, produced by NCSA, who developed the original Mosaic Web browser
http://www.ncsa.uiuc.edu/General/Internet/WWW/ HTMLPrimer.html

The **WWW & HTML Developer's JumpStation**, maintained by SingNet and hosted by OneWorld Information Services, has links to many HTML guides
http://oneworld.wa.com/htmldev/devpage/dev-page1.html#doc-a

Links to **HTML language, tutorials and style guides**
http://union.ncsa.uiuc.edu/HyperNews/get/www/html.html

Here are some tips to help you learn HTML:

1   If you see a page that you like, use the File: Save As option to save a copy on your PC's hard disk. You can then study the HTML codes used and cut and paste them to your own documents.

2   Consider using a specialized HTML editor to create your files – it can save you a lot of effort.

3   When you have gained some experience, create a template file which contains all the HTML codes that will appear on every page, and use it as the basis of your Web pages.

4   It is a good idea to include your contact details on every page you create. This can include links to your department's and organization's Web sites.

There are a number of free services that will automatically check HTML files that you have produced to ensure that they are correct. They will also warn you if you have used browser-specific (ie Netscape) tags. Here is the URL of a UK HTML validation service:
http://www.hensa.ac.uk/html-val-svc/

5.6.1   *Basic HTML features*

These include:

–   six levels of headings (these are not automatically numbered)
–   horizontal rules (lines) across the page to visually divide sections of the document
–   numbered lists (automatically numbered), bulleted lists and definition lists
–   bold, italic and underlined text, as well as teletype font (fixed width, like Courier)
–   hypertext links to other URLs (Web pages, ftp files, gopher menus, etc)
–   hypertext links to specific locations on the same page or on other Web pages
–   in-line (ie within the text) graphics – stored separately as GIF image files
–   codes for accented or European characters – for example, é is **é**
–   HTML codes which define the function of the tagged text – for example, <ADDRESS> for addresses, <BLOCKQUOTE> for quoted text, <PRE> for pre formatted text (eg program code)
–   comments which appear in the HTML file but are not displayed by the browser.

5.6.2   *Creating forms using HTML*

All newer versions of Web browsers understand the HTML codes used to create forms. Your Web server needs additional software to be able to process forms.

You can find information and tutorials on forms at these URLs:

NCSA
http://www.ncsa.uiuc.edu/SDG/Software/Mosaic/Docs/fill-out forms/overview.html

Vlib: the Web Developer's Virtual Library
http://WWW.stars.com/Tutorial/HTML/Forms/

University of Southampton
http://www.soton.ac.uk/devpages/forms/process_form.html

You can include the following forms features:
- fill-in single-line text fields of a specified size
- fill-in multiple-line text fields
- check-boxes
- radio-buttons
- drop-down menus (single or multiple choice)
- scrolling options lists (single or multiple choice)
- **Submit** and **Reset** buttons.

When the reader clicks the **Submit** button, the information they have typed or selected is sent back to the Web server. It can be:
- sent to a specified email address
- passed to a program which processes it in some way – stores it in a database, for instance
- used to retrieve data from a database, which is then sent back to the browser: Internet search tools typically use this method.

Example of form features displayed by Netscape

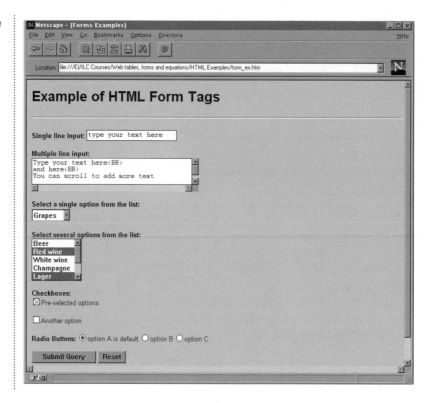

5.6.3 Creating tables using HTML

The latest versions of the Netscape, Microsoft and Mosaic Web browsers can display tables coded using proprietary HTML codes. You can find information and tutorials on tables at these URLs:

Netscape
http://home.netscape.com/assist/net_sites/tables.html

NCSA
http://www.ncsa.uiuc.edu/SDG/Software/Mosaic/Docs/table-spec.html

Vlib: the Web Developer's Virtual Library
http://WWW.stars.com/Tutorial/HTML/Tables/

You can include the following table features:
- borders around all cells and/or the whole table
- controllable border thickness and 'padding' space around data in cells
- specific table and cell widths – expressed in pixels or as a percentage of the Web page's width (which is determined by the size of the browser's window)
- joined cells – horizontally or vertically

- alignment of text within cells
- tables nested within tables
- cells containing any combination of text, images and links.

A simple example of a table displayed by Netscape

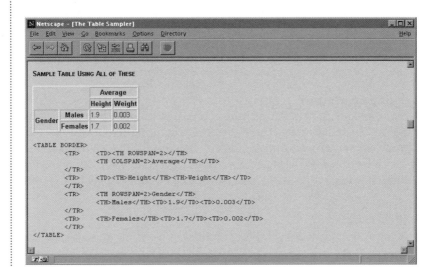

5.6.4 *Images and HTML*

It is easy to include images such as graphics, photos, diagrams, graphs, charts, maps and screen-grabs in Web pages. These images must be stored as GIF (Graphics Interchange Format) files. These use image compression techniques to minimize the size of the file, and support a maximum of 256 colours. GIF files are bitmaps – the picture is essentially a grid of coloured dots (called pixels) like a TV image.

There are several ways to produce GIF image files:

▲ create the image using a graphics program, and save it using a suitable file format – either GIF or another format which can be easily converted to GIF

▲ create the images using another application – for example, all spreadsheets can automatically draw a chart using specified data – and save it using a suitable file format

▲ if the application is unable to save images in any suitable format, take a 'snapshot' of the screen which can then be edited using a graphics program so that it only contains the part you want, and saved using a suitable file format

▲ scan the photo or artwork, and save it using a suitable file format.

Relatively few programs are able to save the images they produce as GIF files, so it is often necessary to convert them to GIFs them using software. You can use powerful (and expensive) image editors such **Adobe Photoshop** to do this, or specialized shareware utilities. The best shareware option for Windows PCs is currently **Paintshop Pro**, with which you can draw, edit, process and convert images.

When you are creating images, take care that they are not too large to display on a typical PC screen (640 pixels wide by 480 pixels high). The maximum practical size is therefore around 600 pixels wide by 400 pixels high – although 300 by 200 (or 200 by 300) pixels is better. Large images can take a long time to retrieve, especially using modem connections to Internet service providers, so don't make images larger than they need to be.

Transparent images

Some image editors, such as Paintshop Pro, are able to save GIFs with one colour defined as 'transparent'. The Web page background colour will show through transparent parts of the image. This is often used with logos to make them look like they are printed on the page rather than enclosed in a box. There are also free utility programs that process GIFs to make one colour transparent, but it is often difficult to specify which colour to make transparent.

JPEG images

Some browsers, such as the latest versions of Netscape and Mosaic, also support images stored as JPEG (Joint Picture Expert Group) files. JPEG files use 24-bit colour (16 million possible colours) as opposed to GIF files, which use 8-bit colour (256 possible colours), so the image quality is higher. They also use a more efficient compression technique than the GIF format, which means that the files are much smaller – typically only one quarter of the number of kilobytes – and this allows faster retrieval across the Web. The JPEG compression technique discards some image detail, but you probably won't notice unless you examine the screen very closely. Users of other (or older) browsers can often configure them so that they will automatically use additional software to view JPEG files.

Image maps

It is possible to create an 'image map' file that associates specific areas of an image with links to URLs. Suppose someone is looking at a Web page that includes a map of the UK showing the location of universities. If they use the mouse to position the screen cursor on Southampton and click, they will follow a link to the University of Southampton's Web page.

These interactive graphics have many uses beyond maps. They are ideal for any application where you want to provide further information on some part of an image – for example a photo of a piece of equipment can have links to other Web pages describing its functions and controls.

Software is available that makes it easy to define areas (circles, rectangles and convex polygons) of an image using interactive tools and link them to specific URLs. The best shareware option for Windows PCs is currently **MapEdit**. Note that the Web server needs additional (free) software to make image maps work.

5.6.5 *Other HTML features*

Many HTML tags have been devised and are supported by Netscape. Use them with caution since they may not be visible to users of other browsers. They enable these features:
– Control over page background colour, text colour, link colour and followed-link colour
– Control over font size – for pieces of text and for the page as a whole
– Textured backgrounds based on small GIF images which are 'tiled' to cover the entire area
– Control over image alignment relative to text
– Control over the appearance of horizontal rules, bulleted lists and list numbering.

Netscape version 2 also supports a new feature called 'frames' which allows several Web pages to be displayed at once, each in its own rectangular area of the browser's window. For example:

Top frame contains logo and Web-site navigation controls	
This frame contains an index of topics available at this Web site	This frame shows the contents of the currently selected topic

Full details are available from Netscape:
http://home.netscape.com/assist/net_sites/index.html
http://home.netscape.com/assist/net_sites/html_extensions.html

5.6.6 *Things you can't yet do using HTML*

Here is a list of features that are difficult to achieve using HTML, plus hints to help you get round the problems:
▲ **Equations and maths characters** You will have to use GIF images.
▲ **Side-by-side columns of text** You can cheat by putting the text in a table without a border – but only Netscape Navigator, Microsoft Internet Explorer and Mosaic 2.0 will display it correctly.

5.7   Web issues

The sudden evolution of the Internet from an academic service into a worldwide commercial marketplace has raised a number of important issues.

5.7.1   Legal aspects

Copyright

Computer technology makes copying information very easy; for example the File: Save As option on your browser enables you to take a copy of anything you find on the Web. But should you? Authors have made their work freely available by publishing it on the Web, but they have not given you permission to copy it. On the other hand, the Web works by transferring copies of files and your browser automatically saves the Web pages you view to a cache on your PC's hard disk. Legally, this is a grey area: you will have to decide for yourself whether storing copies of Web pages is acceptable.

Whatever your decision, you should not republish information from Web pages or conventionally-published material without written permission from the author or publisher. Some people don't think twice about scanning artwork from a magazine or copying a graph from a book to include in their Web pages. You might argue that this casual copying does no harm, but you would not want to have to do so in court!

Libel

Email, mailing lists and Usenet newsgroups make it easy for individuals to send messages to large groups of people. Many organizations therefore fear that they will be held legally responsible if their staff or students send libellous messages. There is not much that can be done about this, apart from alerting email users to the potentially serious results if they libel someone. Some sites check every out-going email message against a list of banned words, but this will only pick out crude abuse rather than malicious allegations. Other problems include activities of hackers (computer experts) who send offensive or libellous email from stolen email accounts, or who fake messages so that they appear to come from someone else.

Obscenity

Sexual morality and censorship vary from one country to another, so the worldwide nature of the Internet poses particular problems. One common concern for parents is that their children may accidentally (or deliberately) come across unsuitable material. It seems likely that commercial sites or Usenet newsgroups carrying pornographic material will adopt a voluntary 'X-rated' tag and that parents and organizations will be able to configure their browsers to disable access to such sites and newsgroups. It is also likely that these commercial sites will restrict access to registered users who will pay for access.

5.7.2 *Technical and commercial matters*

The Internet is creaking under the strain of all the organizations and people who now use it every day. Internet connections to the US slow down to a crawl around lunch-time in the UK – when America starts to wake up. Of course, the commercial nature of the Internet also means that there is now more money being spent on upgrading the physical network, but demand looks likely to outstrip supply for a while yet.

The role of the cable TV companies may be crucial since they have already established fibre-optic networks in many urban areas. There already exist technologies that offer very fast data transfer from the fibre-optic cable to business premises and homes via existing copper phone cabling – but their introduction is still a year or so away.

Encryption will ensure that people's email remains private – although governments still want the key – and that financial transactions can be carried out securely. This will move electronic banking as well as on-line shopping into a new era, and will ensure that the Internet becomes a global marketplace. Free access to information may well decrease as charging for it becomes easier.

Advertising will undergo a revolution too, since people will have to want to look at it. It will have to entertain, educate and inform – as well as sell. Sponsorship of popular sites that provide free access is already taking place.

5.7.3 *Future trends*

In 1992, the World Wide Web was an idea being developed at the CERN physics research facility. Since then it has arguably become the primary means of delivering information across the Internet – with email remaining the primary means of communication.

The capabilities of Web pages are continually being expanded as new HTML codes are devised and new versions of browsers released to take advantage of them. In the past two years HTML has been extended to include fill-in forms, tables, textured backgrounds, coloured text, control of font sizes, etc. Many of these features are supported only by the Netscape browser, but this is typical of the way in which commercial concerns are now setting the pace.

A wave of new technologies now appearing will revolutionize the Web and the way in which it is used:

Java
A programming language developed by Sun Microsystems, Java is used to create small programs that are automatically downloaded and run when you view a Web page. These programs will add animation, sound and interactivity to the page.

New versions of popular Web browsers are being developed which can interpret and run Java code. This means that a Java program will run and produce the same results on Windows PCs, Macintosh and UNIX workstations.

Shockwave

Shockwave enables Netscape to display Web pages that include interactive animations produced using the popular Macromedia Director software. This currently offers the advantage that Director is a well-established tool for creating high quality interactive animations while Java is a new and complex programming language.

VRML

VRML (Virtual Reality Modelling Language) extends the Web to include 3-D interactive environments. Add-on software for Netscape enables you to navigate around these imaginary spaces and interact with the objects they contain. For example, if the VRML environment is a 3-D model of the Earth in space, showing the position of weather satellites, by clicking on one you might retrieve the latest weather picture taken by that satellite.

These technologies, and others, such as video conferencing and shared virtual reality, all require large amounts of data to be transferred. Again, the race by cable TV companies to provide 'video-on-demand' to homes may provide the key that transforms these technologies into mass-market realities.

31246850